W9-ASI-797

DATE DUE

A New Library of the Supernatural
the Supernatural

Enigmas and Mysteries

Enigmas
and Mysteries
by Colin Wilson

Doubleday and Company, Inc.
Garden City, New York, 1976

EDITORIAL CONSULTANTS:

COLIN WILSON
DR. CHRISTOPHER EVANS

Series Coordinator: John Mason
Design Director: Günter Radtke
Picture Editor: Peter Cook
Editor: Mary Senechal
Copy Editor: Mitzi Bales
Research: Frances Vargo
General Consultant: Beppie Harrison

Library of Congress Cataloging in Publication Data
Wilson, Colin 1931 –
Enigmas and Mysteries
(A New Library of the Supernatural)
1. Curiosities and Wonders I. Title II. Series
AG243.W54 001.9'4 76-18373
ISBN 0-385-11321-8

Doubleday and Company
ISBN: 0-385-11321-8

Library of Congress Catalog
Card No. 76-18373

A New Library of the Supernatural
ISBN: 11327

© 1976 Aldus Books Limited, London
D. L.: S.S.: 317/76
Printed and bound in Spain
by TONSA San Sebastián
and RONER Madrid

**Frontispiece: Callanish standing stones in Britain.
Above: statue of Ho-tei, Japanese god of good luck.**

Enigmas and Mysteries

In our 20th-century conceit, we believe we have the answers – if not to all the questions, at least to the important ones. But many curious enigmas continue to mystify and to challenge us. Have we truly defined time and space? Or are there dimensions that are still beyond our present understanding?

Contents

1

Disturbing Contacts

On the afternoon of September 23, 1880 a horse and buggy set out from the small town of Gallatin, Tennessee. The driver, Judge August Peck, had decided to spend the warm and pleasant afternoon visiting his friend David Lang, who owned a farm 12 miles from Gallatin. He was accompanied by Lang's brother-in-law.

A quarter of a mile from the Lang house, Judge Peck turned his buggy into a long lane that ran beside a 40-acre field. A few minutes later he saw David Lang walking across the field. Lang waved, and turned toward the farmhouse a few hundred yards away.

Most of us have the uncomfortable thought that there is more to the world than can be explained by conventional science. Are all the stories of irrational events completely without basis in fact? Above: Charles Fort, who spent his life collecting and assembling accounts of inexplicable things—phenomena that defied rational science. He said that every science is a mutilated octopus—"if its tentacles were not clipped to stumps, it would feel its way into disturbing contacts." Right: *Very Unpleasant Weather*, a 19th-century English cartoon that illustrates the old saying, "It's raining cats, dogs, and pitchforks." Fort was fascinated by the many reports of objects falling from the sky. Could the proverb have arisen from a real "rain" of animals and implements?

"Each day the answering shouts grew fainter"

And then, suddenly, he disappeared from everyone's view. There was a scream from the farmhouse as Mrs. Lang saw her husband disappear. The two Lang children, 8-year-old George and 11-year-old Sarah, were looking across the meadow toward the approaching buggy, so they also witnessed the extraordinary event. A moment later, all five people were running across the field toward the spot where David Lang had vanished. The judge and Lang's brother-in-law expected to find a hole or a crack in the ground, but did not. There was only an unbroken surface hardened by a hot dry Tennessee summer. After a short search, Mrs. Lang began to sob hysterically, and had to be taken back to the house. The others rang the alarm bell that stood in the yard, and neighbors hurried across the fields to see how they could help. They joined in the search, and by nightfall had combed every inch of the meadow. They found not even one clue to the disappearance of David Lang.

The Lang mystery caused a local sensation, and was widely reported in newspapers. The curious and the morbid came to stare at the spot where Lang had last been seen. Mrs. Lang had a breakdown. The servants left, terrified of the silent nights. In sympathy for Mrs. Lang, the local authorities posted guards on the field to turn away the sensation seekers. They also drilled and dug into the soil at the spot where the farmer had vanished, suspecting the existence of underground caves. But they found only solid limestone.

In the following year—one account says in April, another August—the two Lang children walked across the place where their father had vanished, and noticed that the grass in a 20-foot circle was coarse and rank. The cattle had cropped the grass just to the edge of this circle, and no farther. Impulsively Sarah shouted: "Father, are you around?" The boy joined in, and they called again and again to no avail. As they walked away, however, they heard a man's voice shouting "Help!" They rushed to the farmhouse and brought their mother back with them. When she shouted for her husband, his voice—sounding very faraway—answered. But renewed search revealed no fresh clues to his whereabouts. The children went back day after day, shouting to their father, and each day the answering shouts grew fainter. Finally they faded away.

Mrs. Lang rented the farm to Judge Peck on the condition that he leave the 40-acre meadow empty. She hoped that one day her husband might reappear as abruptly as he had vanished, but the hope was vain. No one ever saw or heard David Lang again.

In 1896, sixteen years after Lang's disappearance, the young writer H. G. Wells wrote *The Plattner Story*, a short work of fiction that appeared in a British magazine called *The New Review*. In the story Plattner, a chemistry teacher, experiments with a strange green powder, causes an explosion, and blows himself into "the fifth dimension." Plattner finds himself in a strange shadowy world lit by a green sun. This shadowy world seems to intersect our world at a certain point, as two lines might intersect at an angle. It is peopled by strange creatures, the "Watchers of the Living," who seem to spend their time looking into our world. Fortunately for Plattner, he has kept hold of the bottle containing the explosive powder, and he succeeds in blowing himself back into 19th-century England in which he belonged.

Well's story was pure invention, but it is worth mentioning it because it was the first appearance in popular fiction of the so-called "fifth dimension." Mathematicians had been discussing similar ideas for decades, however. The great Russian mathematician Lobatchevsky, who died in 1856, was the first to suggest that the kind of geometry we learn at school may not be the whole story. For example, the angles of a triangle drawn on the surface of a balloon add up to more than 180 degrees. Another mathematical genius, Bernhard Riemann, even suggested that space itself might be curved, and he developed a

Above: the novelist H. G. Wells. He was the first to present the notion of the "fifth dimension" to a popular audience, which had previously been familiar only with the four traditional dimensions: length, width, depth, and time.

Left: the German physicist Max Planck, who died in 1947. He introduced the Quantum Theory in 1900, a revolutionary concept that has become the foundation of physics in the 20th century. His theory says that light and heat are particles rather than waves. In developing this idea, Planck also found it necessary to invent a geometry in which space is not limited to three dimensions.

Above: Stonehenge. It has been discovered that many sites of ancient importance align along straight lines, called "ley" lines. Researchers have suggested that these ley lines may in fact follow invisible lines of power which criss-cross the country.

Left: the ley line passing through Salisbury to Stonehenge. It links Clearbury Ring, an earthwork; Salisbury Cathedral; the ancient earthwork called Old Sarum; and six miles north, Stonehenge.

Right: a drawing of a stormy Stonehenge by J. M. W. Turner. It has been suggested by proponents of the ley theory that these ancient monuments might serve as condensers of electrical forces, attracting lightning, as depicted.

geometry of curved space. When the physicist Max Planck created the Quantum Theory—which says that light and heat are not waves, but particles or "packages"—he also found it necessary to invent a geometry in which space can have any number of dimensions besides the usual three.

Of course, we cannot even begin to imagine a world with dozens of "dimensions," just as we cannot imagine colors that are not within our limited spectrum. Yet if our eyes could be made sensitive to radiations of longer wavelength than violet, we would see new colors that do not at present exist for us. If such new colors are a known possibility, why couldn't there be new dimensions?

Did David Lang, like Plattner, disappear into the fifth dimension? We have no way of knowing. But it is worth asking the question if only to remind ourselves that, at the time of his disappearance, Lang's relatives could not even conceive such an idea. As far as they could tell, the only explanation that fitted the facts was that Lang had somehow disintegrated like a burst soap bubble. However, this fails to take into account the cries for help heard a year later. We may not yet be able to accept and explain the fifth dimension, but at least we can understand it as a possibility. This may bring us one step closer to solving the enigma of David Lang's disappearance—and of dozens of other strange disappearances.

In the summer of 1906 another 40-acre field was involved in a disappearance case. It was located next to the marshaling yards of the Great Western Railway about a mile from Gloucester in southwest England. Three children of the Vaughan family, a ten-year-old boy and two younger sisters, walked into this field and vanished. For three days crowds of searchers combed every inch of the field and the surrounding countryside. At dawn on the fourth day, a ploughman on his way to work looked over the hedge of the field and saw the children asleep in a ditch. When the children were awakened, they claimed that they remembered nothing of what had happened from the moment they entered the field to the moment they woke up in the ditch. In the late 1940s a researcher interested in strange phenomena sought out the boy in the case, then in his fifties. He verified that he had absolutely no memory of what had taken place.

The official police view at the time was that the children had been kidnapped. They even suspected the ploughman who reported finding them. However, a kidnapping would not explain the children's loss of memory. Besides, the Vaughan family was a poor one with no money for a ransom. And why would a kidnapper go to all the trouble of abducting three children instead of one? The police found no explanation, and the affair remained a mystery.

Harold Wilkins, who had himself taken part in the search for the Vaughan children, wrote about the case in his book *Mysteries, Solved and Unsolved*. He advances the theory that certain places on earth—places associated with witchcraft and ancient rites— are pervaded by strange unknown forces. If so, it could be that the ordinary dimensions of our known physical world are warped or bent in such places. It is then not impossible to imagine a person or animal falling into another dimen-

Above: Jean Baptiste Lamarck, who suggested in 1801 that the present-day animals evolved from primitive ancestors. He used fossils as evidence for his theory.

Right: *Archeopteryx*, one of the most ancient known fossil birds. The traditional scientific view of objects like this fossil was, before the 19th century, that it was simply the remains of a freak of nature, unrelated to creatures now found living in the world.

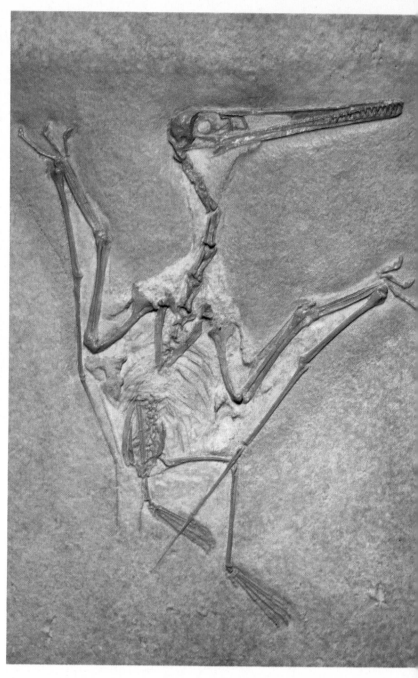

sion and disappearing from three-dimensional space, while remaining alive. Perhaps the two 40-acre fields that swallowed farmer Lang and the Vaughan youngsters were multidimensional. The children fortunately fell out again—but Lang remained trapped.

More recently another hypothesis has been put forward by John Michell, a British writer on the occult. In his book *The View Over Atlantis*, published in 1969, Michell says that the ancient Chinese believed that the earth is covered with lines of magnetic force, which they called *lung-mei*, or dragon paths. They believed that these paths extend over the entire world. Points at which several of the paths meet are "holy centers" invested with particular power, and are frequently marked by mountains, hills, and stone circles. In the 1920s Alfred Watkins, a businessman and amateur archeologist, observed that whole areas of the English countryside are criss-crossed with straight lines, indicating ancient tracks that join hilltops, churches, and prehistoric monuments. He called these lines "leys." Since he first discovered them, hundreds of observers have mapped a system of leys extending all over Britain. Watkins assumed that the leys were merely "old straight tracks." Michell suggests that they are dragon paths joining centers of spiritual power. Two famous sites of ancient worship—the great prehistoric stone circle at Stonehenge, and Glastonbury with its legends of King Arthur and of early Christianity—are the focus of many such paths.

Ley lines also meet in the area around Gloucester where the Vaughan children vanished. Did these mysterious lines of force have anything to do with their disappearance? We do not know. But the very idea may serve to remind us that what appears to be the simplest solution to a problem is not necessarily the most satisfactory or desirable. For example, scientists for many years were aware of the existence of the fossils of prehistoric fishes and animals—creatures that no longer exist. In the 18th century, scientists realized that many of these fossils are found in geological layers that are older than mankind. According to accepted belief, however, the earth had been created in the year 4004 B.C. as demonstrated by Archbishop James Ussher in the previous century. And man was created only seven days later. So most 18th-century scientists chose the "simple" explanation that the fossils were freaks of nature.

Even Baron Cuvier, one of the greats of science and the father of comparative anatomy, preferred the "simple" explanation. He was convinced that Creation had proceeded in four stages, each brought to an end by some tremendous universal catastrophe like the biblical flood. These catastrophes explained why the fossilized animals no longer existed. When a fellow zoologist, Jean Baptiste Lamarck, suggested that all present-day animals have evolved over millions of years, Cuvier was so enraged that he deliberately destroyed Lamarck's career, and the latter died in poverty.

In fact, the theory of evolution is as simple as these other explanations. But in order to understand that, we have to see it as a part of the far larger pattern of the earth and the solar system. Perhaps the solution of the Vaughan children's disappearance is just as simple—and a great deal more plausible— than the notion that they were kidnapped by a local ploughman. But we will not understand it until we have begun to grasp the secret of the underlying pattern.

Lamarck was way ahead of his time. So, in the area of the unexplained, was Charles Hoy Fort, intellectual rebel and hermit who died in New York City in 1932 at the age of 57.

Charles Fort's father was a wealthy businessman who ruled his family with autocratic severity, often beating Charles with a dog-whip. An intelligent and strong-willed child, Fort grew up with a passionate hatred of authority and stupidity. He was always a maverick.

He had always wanted to be a naturalist, and was an eager

Above: Baron Cuvier, who died in 1832. Like many other scientists before and since, he believed firmly in traditional explanations. He was implacably opposed to new ideas and suggestions that ran counter to his preconceived view of the world of nature—expert though he undoubtedly was in the field of comparative anatomy. With the absolute conviction that he was right, he hounded his fellow zoologist Lamarck, who died in great poverty in 1829.

Above: Charles Fort, author and eccentric. He started by taking notes on all sorts of curiosities that attracted his attention. Later he narrowed his field of interest and assembled his vast collection of data that cannot be explained, and thus are ignored.

Above: a 19th-century engraving of a fall of fish. Fort in his *Book of the Damned* lists five such occurrences one after the other, and gives his explanation, "That the bottom of a super-geographical pond had dropped out."

Left: a German engraving of 1670 recording what appears to have been a rain of flaming planks in the French province of Touraine on August 15 that year. It was this kind of peculiar, unexplained event that fascinated Fort. He spent 30 years in the New York Public Library collecting all reports of similar odd phenomena.

collector of specimens. But in his teens he decided to be a writer and took a job on the Albany *Democrat*. He wrote novels—three and a half million words according to his own later estimate—but only one was published. It was a flop. Perhaps it was because Fort writes in a series of brief flat statements, often without verbs. To say that his style lacks flow and readability is an understatement.

In his late teens he traveled around the world on an allowance of $25 a month. After his trip, he married an English girl, and settled in a cheap apartment in New York. He made a poor living from journalism. Later, he received a small income from securities, but life was always a struggle. Fort was an eccentric and a recluse, obsessed by the mysterious and the unexplained from a fairly early age. He devoured books on Atlantis, the hollow earth theory, and the mystery of the pyramids. One of his own earliest books argued that our civilization is secretly controlled from Mars. He called this book simply *X*. Subsequently he wrote a book called *Y*, and planned another called *Z*.

Fort himself was no crank, however. He wrote *X* and *Y* with tongue in cheek, but later he attempted a closely reasoned statement of his beliefs in *The Book of the Damned*, published in 1919. By "damned" he meant phenomena that had been discredited and disregarded by orthodox science—enigmas, unsolved mysteries, the unexplained.

Here is a typical Fort entry:

"Extract from the log of the bark *Lady of the Lake* by Captain F. W. Banner: . . .

"That upon the 22nd of March, 1870, at Lat. 5° 47′ N., Long. 27° 52′ W., the sailors of the *Lady of the Lake* saw a remarkable object, or 'cloud,' in the sky. They reported to the captain.

"According to Capt. Banner, it was a cloud of circular form, with an included semicircle divided into four parts, the central dividing shaft beginning at the center of the circle and extending far outward, and then curving backward.

"Geometricity and complexity and stability of form: and the small likelihood of a cloud maintaining such diversity of features, to say nothing of appearance of organic form.

"Light gray in color, or it was cloud-color.

"That whatever it may have been, it traveled against the wind . . .

"For half an hour this form was visible. When it did finally disappear that was not because it disintegrated like a cloud, but because it was lost to sight in the evening darkness."

This might make the reader think at once of a flying saucer, especially since Captain Banner's description sounds like hundreds of other UFO sightings. But Fort recorded this account in 1918, thirty years before the start of the UFO craze. He was merely quoting from the *Journal of the Royal Meteorological Society*, an eminently respectable publication. He makes no attempts to draw conclusions from the report. It is simply one of hundreds of similar unexplainable occurrences that he quotes at length and in detail.

We can see immediately why Fort's contemporaries regarded him as mildly if not certifiably insane. Fort spent 30 years of his

The Riddle of the Pools of Fish

An earthquake. A deluge of rain. Dead fish in dried up pools all over town. This weird sequence of events happened in Singapore in 1861. The description of it in *La Science Pour Tous* said the fish had not fallen with the rain. The local inhabitants of Singapore said they had. Charles Fort, American writer on the occult, supported the view that the fish had fallen from the sky. He thought "that a whole lakeful of them [fish] had been shaken down from the Super-Sargasso Sea."

Fort spent his life collecting scraps of information about odd, hard-to-explain occurrences everywhere in the world. He used such bits in his various books, which he wrote as his personal protest against modern science's failure to deal with psychic phenomena.

In *The Book of the Damned*, published in 1919, Fort talks about Singapore's puddles of fish as an example of things falling from the sky. He says that many such falling objects come from the Super-Sargasso Sea. According to Fort, this sea is a "region somewhere above the earth's surface in which gravitation is inoperative. . . ." He goes on to say, "I think that things raised from this earth's surface to that region have been held there until shaken down by storms—"

The Flying Hay

People in the Welsh town of Wrexham and the surrounding countryside were startled to see hay flying under its own power one ordinary summer day in the late 19th century.

According to an account carried in an English newspaper, the event occurred at 2 p.m. on a July day. It was an exceptionally calm day so that the wind was unlikely to pick objects up and whirl them about.

Suddenly some haymakers on a farm near Wrexham saw about half a ton of hay sailing above them through the sky. They said it was higher than they had even seen a crow fly.

The flying hay moved in a northerly direction, which was somewhat surprising because it was going against the wind. Although the mass separated slowly as it covered more distance, it traveled at least five miles without falling apart entirely. It had risen from a field about five miles from Wrexham and had flown over that town at some point in its flight. As the article said, "it caused much consternation while passing over the town."

At the end of this flight of hay, wisps lay here and there along its route. One large clump fell in the middle of a field some distance from the point at which the half-ton mass had first taken to the sky.

life in the New York Public Library, searching through piles of old newspapers and magazines for items like the one quoted above. He was particularly fond of tales of odd things falling from the sky—frogs, fish, blood, and snowflakes two-feet square. But what did it all add up to? Why should Fort spend a lifetime assembling a vast collection of tall stories and make no attempt to tie them together into a theory?

The flying saucer story above provides the answer. Fort could be described as a man of inspired intuition. He was also, by upbringing and training, a typical product of the age that believed in hard work, sound common sense, and respect for authority. All his instincts told him there was something wrong with the neat and orderly universe of science, and that the actual universe was a million times stranger than even the most brilliant scientist of his day could imagine. It was this instinct that rang a bell when he read the flying saucer story and dozens more like it—although he would have found it difficult to explain precisely why. In a sense, he wasn't even interested in explaining these phenomena. He felt there could be dozens of possible explanations, all equally at variance with scientific thinking, all equally exciting and fruitful.

Here is a typical example of the kind of thing that interested him. On July 28, 1860, fifteen years before Fort's birth, a great meteorite covered with ice crashed down in Dhurmsalla, India. The event was duly noted and described by a trustworthy authority, the British Deputy Commissioner in the area. An

Above: the cover of *Lo!*, Fort's third book. Tiffany Thayer, one of Fort's few friends, suggested the title, he says, "because in the text the astronomers are forever calculating and then pointing to the sky where they figure a new star or something should be and saying 'Lo!'—and there's nothing whatever to be seen where they point." Fort agreed to the suggested title at once.

Above: a double white rainbow, an example of a typically Fortean curiosity. In this case there is a scientific explanation: it is seen when the size of the droplets making up the rainbow is very small, of a diameter of 0.1 mm. or less. It is known as Ulloa's ring. Below: a rain of crosses that was reported in 1094, shown in this contemporary woodcut. Fort found and recorded several accounts of falls of tiny crosses. He adds, "But some are Roman crosses, some St. Andrew's, some Maltese."

Above: a 19th-century engraving of the peculiar atmosphere when on May 19, 1780 the northeast United States was plunged into a darkness that lasted 15 hours. Fort collected many instances when intense darkness covered areas, much as eclipses occur, but which were not referable to any known eclipsing body. Fort suggested the cause might be "the proximity of other worlds."

ice-covered meteorite is certainly strange, since most meteorites are white hot from tearing through our atmosphere. That was not all. On the next evening the Commissioner saw lights in the sky, some of them fairly low. They moved around like fire balloons. Nowadays we would probably assume they were the lights of airplanes, but this was long before the invention of the airplane. Fort also noticed from the Commissioner's report that other unusual events had occurred around the same time in India. Newspapers had reported a shower of live fish at Benares, a fall of some red substance at Farrukhabad, a dark spot observed on the sun, an earthquake, a lengthy period of darkness during daylight hours, and a luminous effect in the sky like the aurora borealis.

In the following year on February 16, 1861 there was an earthquake in Singapore, followed by a tremendous storm with three days of torrential rain. The odd thing was that in the pools of water formed by the rain, fish were seen swimming around; and when the pools dried up, dead fish were found on the ground. The most popular theory was that the heavy rain had caused a river to overflow, spreading the fish over a wide area. However, a reporter of the event recorded that fish were found in his courtyard, which was surrounded by a high wall that kept the water out.

Here Fort offers a strange, mixed mass of data, some baffling, some fairly straightforward. There is nothing unusual in a sunspot, or in the aurora borealis effect that followed it. The lights in the sky could in fact have been fire balloons or ball lightning, although the Commissioner stated that he was sure they weren't. As to the rain of red substance and the falling fish, it seems just conceivable that they were carried aloft by a whirlpool or waterspout. Fort agrees that all these explanations could be true, but argues that there must be something more when so many strange events occur together. "My own acceptance is that either a world or a vast super-construction . . . hovered over India in the summer of 1860," he says. As to the lights in the sky, his suggestion is: "Visitors." One of his general conclusions is that the earth has had many "visitors" at various times in its history.

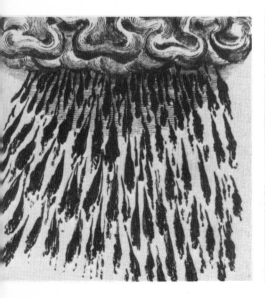

Above: a photograph of ball lightning taken in August 1961,
which appeared to cause a small explosion. Such unusual but
"normal" phenomena might well have provided the foundation for
some accounts of strange lights in the sky that Fort collected.
Far left: a rain of blood, reported to have taken place in
Lisbon in 1551, which apparently terrified the inhabitants.
Left: blood-red rain which fell on England and Wales during the
night of June 30, 1968, seen on the windshield and hood of a car.
Meteorologists explained it as the result of fine sand being picked
up in the Sahara in dust storms and carried northward in the upper
air. It is calculated that 10 million tons of sand fell in the thun-
dery rain that night. Britain also had a red rain like this in 1903.
Right: a cover of *Doubt* magazine, published by The Fortean
Society from 1937 to 1959 when Tiffany Thayer, editor and the
moving spirit behind the Society, died. His description of this
cover was that it was "a spirit drawing showing Charles Fort on
the Other Side. He has clearly dethroned the Hebrew Yahweh
('God' to you) and taken possession of Jupiter's thunderbolts."

doubt

THE
FORTEAN
SOCIETY
MAGAZINE

No. 20

EDITED BY   25c

TIFFANY THAYER

Above: Jacques Bergier, French scientific writer who is also well known for his books on unexplained phenomena. In 1960 the book he had written with Louis Pauwels, *The Morning of the Magician*, became a best seller. It contained a chapter on Fort, and it rekindled interest in him.

As to what kind of visitors: "I can think of as many different kinds of visitors to this earth as there are visitors to New York, to a jail, to a church—some people go to church to pick pockets."

Fort likes to keep all his options open. That is why he refuses to commit himself to any single theory to explain all the strange events he writes about. He always has half-a-dozen possible solutions for everything. Perhaps our earth passed through an area of space where there were shattered fragments of some other world. Perhaps "super-vehicles" have traveled through our atmosphere. (This seems to make Fort the inventor of the UFO hypothesis.) Perhaps there is some *other* world—a kind of twin to this one—in another dimension. Or perhaps all these theories are wide of the mark, and the truth is that "all things are phantoms in a super-mind in a dreaming state." Just as you are beginning to feel that perhaps Fort is building up to some plausible scientific theory after all, he reaches into his hat like a conjuror and produces some new and even more outrageous hypothesis. For example, he suggests that human beings may be "property" belonging to some invisible super-farmer. He seems to *want* his readers to lose patience and throw the book across the room.

As could be expected, most of Fort's contemporaries ignored him, and he repaid their neglect with contempt. When the writer Tiffany Thayer launched a Fortean Society in his honor, Fort firmly declined to become a member. He probably feared that his disciples would try to pin him down to a definite set of ideas and beliefs, and he had no intention of being pinned down.

For day after day and year after year, Fort continued his obsessive search through the world's newspapers, making endless notes on slips of paper which he kept in shoe boxes. After *The Book of the Damned* came *New Lands*, then *Lo!*, and finally *Wild Talents*. Fort became more and more of a hermit. He spent the morning in the library, and the afternoon at his desk, working in a small dark room that overlooked a courtyard. Almost his only recreation was going to the movies in the neighborhood four or five times a week, and he said he went to keep his wife company. For himself, most films "bored him to death."

While Fort was writing *Wild Talents* his health began to break down—understandably in view of his dreary and frustrating existence. He wrote desperately, often sending his wife to the movies alone and joining her later. The recluse became intensely resentful of all visitors, refusing to see anyone. He would not even consult a doctor. Finally, Fort became so weak that his wife had to send for an ambulance and take him to the hospital. But he had finished his book. When the publisher brought a copy of *Wild Talents* to the hospital, Fort was too weak to hold it. He died later the same day.

Fort was ignored in death as in life. Although the Fortean Society continued, it was composed of a small group of eccentrics. They admired Fort's fierce individualism, but if members of the general public picked up Fort's books, they soon dropped them again. Fort seldom bothers to tell a complete story. He breaks off halfway through some anecdote about giants or fairies or spontaneous combustion to denounce orthodox scientists or to hector the reader. He simply dumps his many facts like a cartload of stones, and leaves the reader to sort them out. This may be why Fort remained unread, and almost unremembered, for a quarter of a century after his death.

An event of 1947 led to Fort's resurrection. In that year an American businessman flying his private plane near Mount Rainier, Washington, saw nine gleaming disks hurtling at tremendous speed through the sky. Within months many more sightings of flying saucers had been reported, and within a few years there were thousands of reports from all over the world. Even then, few people remembered Fort, pioneer of the UFO idea. In France, however, Fort had at least one ardent admirer. This was Jacques Bergier, a student of philosophy and occultism. Bergier was fascinated by unexplained enigmas such as the riddle of the pyramids, the Easter Island statues, and evidence for highly evolved civilizations in the remote past. In the late 1950s Bergier teamed up with a brilliant journalist, Louis Pauwels, and together they produced the book that Fort had attempted to write all his life. They called it *The Morning of the Magicians*. When it appeared in Paris in 1960, it became an immediate best-seller. It contained a chapter about Charles Fort, and acknowledged its indebtedness to him. Published in Britain and the United States in 1963, it inspired hundreds of imitators. Secondhand works on Atlantis, magic, pyramidology, alchemy, and astrology began to get record prices. Publishers realized there was an "occult boom," and began to flood the market with titles like *World of the Weird* and *Nothing So Strange*. All Fort's books were reissued in paperback, and translations appeared all over the world. Recognition had finally arrived—half a century too late.

Many people now regard Fort as a prophet and a visionary, and many of his ideas have become part of the intellectual currency of our time. Today we freely discuss the possibility of a multidimensional universe in which other worlds could exist parallel with ours. The idea of visitors from other worlds has become commonplace in the past two decades. Arthur C. Clarke's *2001* suggested that human evolution may have been aided by beings from another galaxy—an idea that has become part of contemporary mythology. The Russian philosopher Georgei Gurdjieff, who has attained the status of a cult figure, liked to describe human beings as hypnotized sheep kept stupid and contented by some magician until it is time for the slaughterhouse. Another cult figure, the Argentinian writer and Nobel Prize winner Jorge Luis Borges, has often speculated that human beings are dreams in the mind of God—and that perhaps God himself is a dream in some even more civilized mind. In recent years, some scientists have suggested that there could be another universe of "antimatter" in which the atoms would be made up of antiprotons, antineutrons, and antielectrons. If ever such a universe were to come into contact with our own, there would be a dull explosion—and then Nothing.

Fort once said that every science is a mutilated octopus. "If its tentacles were not clipped to stumps, it would feel its way into disturbing contacts." Forty years after the death of Charles Fort, it seems that we may at last be entering the age of what he called disturbing contacts.

Below: Jorge Luis Borges, the Argentinian poet who has become a cult figure partly because of his cosmic speculations. He has conjectured that God might only be a dream in the mind of some unfathomable supercivilized being.

Strange Disappearances

In December 1937 China and Japan had been at war for six months, and the Chinese were getting the worst of the struggle. Shanghai fell, and in spite of the protests of the League of Nations, the Japanese advanced on the capital of Nanking.

South of the city, the Chinese commander Colonel Li Fu Sien decided to make a last-ditch stand in the low hills. An urgent request brought over 3000 reinforcements. The colonel disposed these troops in a two-mile line, close to an important bridge across the Yangtze River. They had a quantity of heavy artillery, and were prepared for a life-and-death struggle. The

There is a pat phrase for it: "He vanished into thin air." But does it happen? Can it possibly happen? Right: a science fiction magazine illustration showing flying saucers evacuating the whole population of Angkor, Cambodia, site of the world-famous Angkor Wat temple. The ancient city was completely abandoned in 1431, and historians have never discovered why. Believers in UFOs say that visitors from another planet removed the people of Angkor, and offer the space-visitor theory to explain other unexplained events.

SPACE SHIPS AT ANGKOR WAT?

Was it really a fleet of space ships that came to Angkor Wat and removed its population to another planet? Anyway, its people could not have vanished more completely than if this had been a reality!

"The entire file of men disappeared"

colonel returned to his headquarters a mile behind the lines, and waited for the Japanese attack. At dawn he was awakened by his aide, who told him that they were unable to contact the army. Had they been overrun by the Japanese in the night? The colonel and an escort drove cautiously toward the right flank to investigate. To their amazement, the positions were deserted. The guns were still in position—but the men had vanished. Further investigation revealed that a small pocket of soldiers, about a hundred, were still encamped near the bridge. They had heard no sounds in the night. If the army had deserted or surrendered to the Japanese, they would have had to pass close to the camp. The sentries on the bridge also testified that no one had crossed the bridge in the night.

It was preposterous. Three thousand men cannot vanish into thin air. Even if they had all deserted, such a mass exodus would have been bound to attract attention. Yet no one had heard or seen anything.

The Chinese had little time to ponder the problem. The Japanese army advanced across the river, and two days later Nanking fell. There followed one of the most horrifying and cruel massacres in history—the "rape of Nanking." The atrocities were so appalling that three Japanese commanders were recalled to Japan, as were many soldiers. The "vanishing army" ceased to be a matter of central importance to the Chinese generals. But it was generally expected that the mystery would be solved when peace returned—that perhaps the solution lay in the records of the Japanese army. In fact, the Japanese army reports contained no mention of the missing 3000 men. Today they are regarded as mysterious casualties of war. But no one knows what became of them.

Why has this mystery failed to excite more attention? The answer is probably that the misery and chaos of the Sino-Japanese war made it seem unimportant. The same seems to apply to an equally strange event that took place during World War I.

In April 1915 Allied armies landed on the Gallipoli Peninsula in European Turkey in an attempt to capture what is now Istanbul, the capital of the Turkish Empire. They wanted to make contact with Russian allies through the Black Sea. It was bad strategy. Turkish resistance was stubborn, and the Allies were forced to withdraw nine months later, having lost hundreds of thousands of men.

Some of the bloodiest fighting in Gallipoli took place around a spot called Hill 60 near Suvla Bay. On the morning of August 28, 1915 a British regiment, the First Fourth Norfolk, prepared to attack Hill 60. The regiment consisted of more than a thousand men. It was a warm, clear day, but several observers remember noticing a group of curious low clouds over Hill 60. Although there was a breeze, these clouds seemed to remain stationary. The observers reported watching the regiment march uphill until the entire file of men disappeared into one of these "loaf shaped" clouds. Then the clouds moved away—leaving no sign of the army.

The disappearance of the regiment was duly reported to the British Government by the Commander-in-Chief of the

Above: Japanese tanks moving into Nanking during the war with China in 1937. Two days before, 3000 Chinese soldiers called up to defend the city had disappeared as though they had never existed.

Left: a soldier by a rough grave in Gallipoli in 1915. During the appallingly bitter fighting in the area, the First Fourth battalion of the Norfolk regiment—several hundred men—apparently vanished.

Right: Jacques Vallée, French writer and researcher in the fields of artificial satellites and computing science, and a believer in the possibility of UFOs. He reports that the battalion may have been captured by a UFO hovering in clouds hanging over the hill.

Allied Expeditionary Force in Gallipoli. He made no mention of the mysterious clouds, but reported that the regiment had separated from the main body of troops and had vanished. The whole regiment was subsequently posted as "missing"—the assumption being that all its men had either been killed or taken prisoner. When the war ended in 1918 the British asked the Turks about their missing regiment. The Turks replied that they knew nothing about it. Their armies had never made contact with the First Fourth Norfolk.

In 1920 the bodies of a number of soldiers belonging to the First Fourth Norfolk were found in Gallipoli. It was assumed that these men must have died in battle after all, and that the remainder of the regiment probably perished in Turkish prisoner-of-war camps. Today it is generally accepted that the men of the First Fourth Norfolk were victims of a bloody campaign in which all too many men were lost without trace.

Some people, however, have never accepted this explanation—particularly the witnesses who recalled the strange clouds over Hill 60. The French writer Jacques Vallée was sufficiently curious to investigate the matter, and included the incident in his book *Passport to Magonia*. He used a letter signed by three witnesses attesting to the curious disappearance of the whole regiment into a cloud.

Vallée is a scientist connected with Northwestern University in Chicago. He has also written one of the most balanced books on Unidentified Flying Objects, *Anatomy of a Phenomenon*. Vallée puts forward the idea that the regiment marched into a cloud that concealed a UFO. This view is supported by the distinguished British ufologist Brinsley Le Poer Trench, now the Earl of Clancarty, who is Chairman of the International UFO Movement. Le Poer Trench cites another cloud disappearance in the curious case of Dr. and Mrs. Gerardo Vidal. They were driving home from a family reunion in Chascomus, Argentina when they drove into a thick cloud of mist. They fell unconscious—and woke to find themselves on a road near Mexico City, 4500 miles away. On telephoning friends in Argentina, they discovered that they had apparently lost two days since they left the party.

This is not the only case in which couples have been *teleported*—that is, moved from one place to another by psychic means—to Mexico. Marcilo Ferraz, the owner of a sugar firm in Brazil, was driving with his wife from São Paulo to Uruguay. Near the border they drove into a white cloud; they woke up to find themselves in Mexico. In 1968 a Brazilian couple, driving through the state of Rio Grande do Sul on their honeymoon, suddenly became extremely drowsy. When they woke up, they were in Mexico.

At this point it is worth mentioning the strange experience of Betty and Barney Hill. It aroused widespread interest, and was the subject of a book, *The Interrupted Journey*, by John G. Fuller. Driving from Canada to New Hampshire in September 1961, the Hills saw a bright object like a star descending through the sky. Looking at the object through binoculars, Barney Hill thought it to be some kind of spacecraft. The couple drove off at high speed, but began to feel drowsy. They woke up an hour later, with no memory of what had happened in the meantime.

When they realized that they had apparently lost an hour—not to mention 35 miles—the Hills feared that they were going insane and began consulting doctors. Dr. Benjamin Simons, a neurosurgeon, helped them recall what had happened during the lost hour by hypnotizing each of them. Their stories under hypnosis were the same. The engine of the Hills' car had failed on the approach of a UFO. They had been taken aboard the craft by beings unlike humans, and had each been subjected to a medical examination. Finally they had been put back in their car, farther along the road, and the memory of what had taken place erased from consciousness.

The story told by the Hills is supported by medical evidence, so it seems unlikely that they were lying. On the other hand, it is possible that the story they told under hypnosis may have been the product of subconscious fantasy—a kind of dream. A couple driving a long distance throughout the night are likely to become drowsy during which time they seem to lose minutes or even hours. It is true that the Hills were hypnotized separately; but it is conceivable that they had discussed the possibility of being kidnapped by extraterrestrial beings before they consulted Dr. Simon, and produced a story based on their discussion under hypnosis. In short, the flying saucer theory remains no more than a hypothesis to explain these strange cases of teleportation even though it seems as plausible as any other hypothesis.

One curious aspect of teleportation incidents is that they so often involve couples. I have myself discussed such an experience with a couple that went through it—Dr. Arthur Guirdham, former Consultant Psychiatrist to the Bath Medical Area in southwest England, and his wife Mary. The Guirdhams were taking a vacation on the Yorkshire moors, and were staying at a hotel in a small town. One day they visited a town some 15 miles away. At the end of the outing, they started to drive back to their hotel. It was a warm pleasant evening, and they drove slowly. They had only been driving for five minutes when Guirdham noticed a signpost that indicated they were only three miles from their destination. This was clearly impossible unless they had been driving at more than a hundred miles an hour. They stopped to consult a map to see if they had taken a short cut or mistaken the distance. They had not. If the signpost were right, then, they had covered 12 miles in less than five minutes. And the signpost was right. A few miles farther on the Guirdhams entered the town where their hotel was situated.

There is a matter-of-factness about this story that argues for its truth. Guirdham did not attempt to draw any conclusions from the incident, or use it as the foundation for an argument about time. He simply recounted it as something odd that had once happened to him. His wife Mary confirmed it.

In this case, there was no question of lost time; it was only the distance that had apparently been telescoped. Which brings us to a fundamental question: is it conceivable that space and time could be stretched or compressed like a piece

The Case of the Transported Soldier

It was a bright October morning in 1593. On the plaza in front of the palace in Mexico City there was the usual bustle of people and soldiers. One of these army men stood out. He wore a resplendent uniform unlike the others, and he carried a different kind of gun.

When questioned later, the strange soldier said that his orders that morning were to mount guard at the governor's palace in Manila, where he was stationed. "I know very well this is not the governor's palace—and evidently I am not in Manila," he said. . . . "But here I am and this is a palace of some kind so I am doing my duty as nearly as possible." The soldier also told the authorities that the governor had been killed the night before.

The soldier couldn't believe that he was thousands of miles away from Manila, and everyone was baffled by his overnight transportation to Mexico City. The man with this incredible tale was put in jail.

Two months afterward a ship arrived from the Philippines. It brought news that the governor had been murdered—on the night before the soldier had appeared. The soldier was released and sent back to Manila. Some 400 years later his marvelous trip through space and time remains a mystery.

Right: Barney and Betty Hill in a hypnotic trance. Hypnosis was used on them separately in an attempt to discover what happened during the time they apparently lost returning from Canada to their home in New Hampshire in 1961. The tale they both told under hypnosis was strange to say the least. It was that they had been taken aboard a UFO, examined like laboratory animals, and then returned to their waiting car.

Right: an artist's impression, using the Hills' descriptions, of one of the creatures that kidnapped and examined them during their strange experience.

of chewing gum? This is a question that will be raised by many of the enigmas and mysteries recounted in this book, and it may be as well to consider it a little more closely.

In his famous book *An Experiment With Time*, first published in 1927, the British aeronautical engineer J. W. Dunne described how he began having dreams of the future. Among them were dreams of newspaper headlines that appeared the day after he dreamed them. Dunne decided to make a habit of jotting down his dreams when he awoke during the night because he was convinced that many interesting dreams are simply forgotten by the time we wake up in the morning. His records confirmed that he often dreamed of events which later happened. He persuaded others to write down their dreams, and they also found that they dreamed of future events that came true. As a result of these experiences, Dunne formulated his theory of "serial time." He suggested that there are several different kinds of time, and several different "me's" on different levels of being. For example, there is the superficial "me" who runs to catch trains, and chats with people at parties; a deeper "me" who appreciates music and poetry; and a still deeper "me" who may be aroused by some great crisis or challenge; and so on. Each of these "me's," Dunne suggests, may have a different kind of time. A simple way to grasp this idea would be to imagine a carousel that contains several different carousels one inside the other, with each one going at a different speed: A different "you" exists on each of the carousels. Because of the speed differences, the "you" on an inner carousel may actually be ahead of the "you" on the outer carousel. Therefore you know what will happen tomorrow, or next week, or even next year.

Dunne's theory has been strongly criticized by many scientists and parapsychologists. Nevertheless it does seem to fit in with those strange glimpses into the future that provide such a challenge to investigators of psychic phenomena. A simple version of Dunne's theory is that time is like a phonograph record, and our human consciousness is like the needle that has to track it. Occasionally the needle can skip a groove, or even several grooves, and jump into the future.

There seems to be a likely possibility that time may be more complex than it looks. But how about space? All our experience tells us that space is the same everywhere. Things *in* space can change, but isn't space itself unchangeable?

The idea of unchangeable space was first challenged in the early years of the 20th century by Albert Einstein. Although it has been said that only a handful of people fully understand Einstein's Theory of Relativity, its implications caught the imagination of the whole world. The first part of Einstein's theory, the Special Theory of Relativity, was published in 1905. It was concerned with bodies traveling at speeds that approached the enormous speed of light. At such speeds, Einstein suggested, measurements of distance and time would be altered: objects would shrink in length· and time would slow down. For instance, a spaceship traveling at half the speed of light—about 93,000 miles per *second*—would have only about 85 percent of its length when at rest, and clocks

Above: Dr. and Mrs. Arthur Guirdham, who discovered during a leisurely drive between two towns 15 miles apart that distance had apparently been telescoped. They covered 12 miles of country roads in less than five minutes.

Where Did the Balloon Go?

Walter Powell was an English politician who was the Member of Parliament for a Wiltshire area. On December 10, 1881 he became part of an unsolved mystery when he went up in a balloon with two of his friends. They came down on a beach in Dorset, the two got out, and Powell started to follow. Suddenly the balloon gave a violent jerk and went high up into the clouds again with Powell still on board. He was never seen again.

It seemed likely that he might have crashed into the English Channel, and a search was made for three days. The beaches on England's southern coast were combed for clues night and day. Nothing helpful turned up anywhere.

Right after Powell's disappearance, reports of mystifying lights and objects in the sky came from England, France, Scotland, and Spain. The day after Powell and the balloon had vanished, people in Dartmouth Harbor saw "two strange bright lights in the sky." Two days later an unidentified luminous object was seen traversing the sky over Cherbourg, France.

On December 15 a ship's captain saw a glowing object in the sky. He described it as the "gondola of a balloon, which seemed alternately to increase and diminish in size." That was in the east of Scotland. On the 16th, three Spanish coastguards reported seeing something that looked like a balloon in the sky. They climbed the nearby mountain to investigate, and saw it shoot out sparks as it vanished. The next day about 75 miles east of this sighting, a similar and strangely glowing object was reported.

Could these unusual sightings have had a connection with Powell's lost balloon?

on board would run at 85 percent of their normal rate. The crew inside the spaceship would even age more slowly because the clocks were slowed down. The crew would not be aware of these effects, however, because everything on the spaceship would be equally affected. On the other hand, the crew looking at the Earth would find that *it* was contracted, and would assume that Earth clocks were running slow compared with theirs. Time slows down on a moving object, and speeds, time intervals, and length are relative to the observer who is measuring them, said Einstein.

The effects of motion on the measurements of time and distance cannot be detected at everyday speeds, but it is impossible for a human being to move at anything like the speed of light. In 1961, however, scientists in Geneva succeeded in accelerating a tiny particle called a *meson* to three-quarters the speed of light. The usual lifespan of this particle, when at rest, is only two-millionths of a second; but at three-quarters the speed of light, the meson lasted three-millionths of a second, or half again as long. This experiment justified Einstein's conclusion that time slows down on a moving object.

Einstein went on to develop the General Theory of Relativity with the aim of explaining gravitation. According to the General Theory, any mass tends to distort or "bend" space itself. The larger the mass, the greater the bending, so the distortion of space around a very large mass like a planet is

considerable. As a result of such distortion, bodies tend to move toward each other in precisely the way bodies are attracted to each other by gravity. The General Theory demonstrated that gravity was a property of the "shape" of space itself.

This theory led to some surprising predictions. According to Einstein's reasoning, light rays ought to bend slightly as they pass close to a large mass like the sun. Many scientists dismissed this idea as absurd. Then in 1919 a total eclipse of the sun made it possible to measure light rays passing close to it from distant stars. It was discovered that light did bend in the sun's gravitational field.

Einstein saw space and time as being somehow bound together into a unity called space-time. If we were able to step outside our Universe and look in, we might see the Universe as a gigantic ball of space-time. Moreover, we would notice that it was more curved in the region of any large mass like a star or a planet.

The Theory of Relativity is extremely complex, and can only be fully understood with the aid of mathematical formulas. However, what matters from our point of view is that scientific research strongly suggests that the theory is correct, and that the space and time which we take for granted are far stranger than we think. A striking illustration of this is the recently advanced theory of so-called "black holes." This holds that

Above: J. W. Dunne (center, in 1919), the British engineer who developed theories of time that have intrigued many investigators.

Left: the eruption of Mount Pelée, Martinique, May 8, 1902. It was this eruption, which Dunne saw prefigured in a dream when he was in South Africa thousands of miles away, that helped convince him that there was some way in which his dreaming caught glimpses of future events. It led him to consider the whole nature of time.

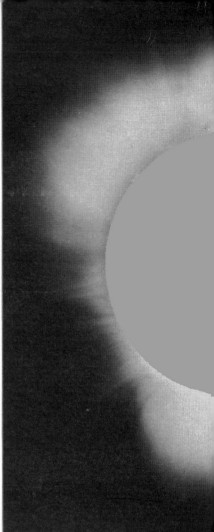

Above: Albert Einstein. The revolutionary Theory of Relativity that he developed changed scientific concepts of both space and time.

Above right: the solar corona during a total eclipse of the sun, photographed at Green River, Wyoming, June 8, 1918. According to Einstein's reasoning, light rays should bend slightly when passing a large mass like the sun. This eclipse provided proof that light did in fact bend.

Right: an artist's impression of a black hole—a collapsed star. The hot radiating gas glows red as the star implodes into the black hole, producing a gravitational field so strong that even light would not escape from it.

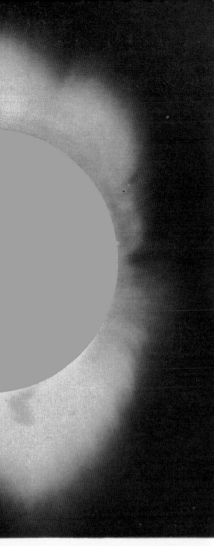

certain stars burned themselves out like giant atom bombs, collapsed in on themselves, and became ever smaller and denser. Afterward their gravitational fields got stronger. It is possible that the pressures exerted by a collapsing star could be so tremendous that it would go on collapsing forever, forming a black hole in space. The gravitational field would be so strong that not even light could escape from it. Anything that fell into a black hole would never get out again—any spaceship or planet that got sucked into this whirlpool of destruction could never escape.

Ideas like these fail to make sense in terms of the world we see around us. Yet there are certain spots on the surface of our Earth where we may be able to gain some impression of the strange effects of space-time. For example, on the banks of Sardine Creek, Oregon, there is a spot known as the "Oregon Vortex." It is about 165 feet across, and the force of gravity seems to be intensified toward its center. Compasses and other instruments refuse to work in the vortex, and a photographer's light meter reveals a considerable difference in intensity between the daylight in the circle and that outside. There is a hut in the vortex—an old office abandoned long ago. It has slipped downhill, and is now at a slight angle toward the center of the circle. People who step into the hut experience a weird sense of unbalance, as if they were in a hall of distorted mirrors at a fairground. This feeling is not entirely an illusion. A ball dangling from a beam in the ceiling of the hut seems to incline toward the center of the vortex. Observations made from outside the vortex prove that this is so. Visitors feel pulled toward the center of the circle, and seem compelled to lean backward at an angle. Cigarette smoke in the vortex spirals upward in a strange manner, and handful of confetti whirls around as if caught in a twister.

It has been suggested that the phenomena of the vortex are due to electromagnetism, but they could equally be the manifestation of some eccentricity in the laws of gravity. Add to this the idea that "waves" of space-time are not fixed, but roll across the universe in a definite rhythm, and we begin to see how certain spots could be freakish and unpredictable. We cannot understand much about their mechanism, but we can see that such a space-time warp could have strange consequences for anyone who happened to get caught in it. Like David Lang, who disappeared in full view of his wife and children. Like the Spanish soldier who was teleported from the Philippines to Mexico City. Or like Benjamin Bathurst, the British Ambassador to the court of Francis I of Austria, who, in the presence of his secretary and valet, strolled around the post horses that were to carry him back to London, and simply vanished. This happened on November 25, 1809—and Bathurst was never seen again. The British suspected that their arch-enemy Napoleon was behind the disappearance, but Napoleon flatly denied knowing anything about it. He might have pointed out that even his secret police had no power to make a man vanish into thin air in front of two witnesses.

Charles Fort mentions the Benjamin Bathurst case, among many other strange disappearances, but has no explanation to

The Home With a Hum

The home of Eugene Binkowski of Rotterdam, New York, had a hum that never stopped. The family wasn't sure when it had started, but became aware of it after a series of illnesses had afflicted each of them. Not only did they have frequent headaches, earaches, and toothaches, but they also suffered from stiffness of the joints. Finally they realized that the source of the problems was a constant faint humming sound throughout the house. They reported the trouble to the police, who could not come up with any explanation.

It was natural that General Electric in nearby Schenectady should become interested in the sound mystery, so the next investigators were technicians from that firm. Using the latest equipment that they had at their command, they tested the house thoroughly. At the end of it, they claimed they could hear no sound of a peculiar nature in the house.

In desperation Binkowski wrote to then President John Kennedy. A few days later some Air Force sound experts turned up with equipment designed to detect high frequency sounds. They could not trace the hum. The only bit of information they offered was that tests showed the whole family had especially acute hearing. It was possible, they said, for the Binkowskis to be hearing a sound at some unusual pitch. Despite the verdicts of the General Electric and Air Force experts, hundreds of visitors to the Binkowski home reported they could hear the hum. Some of them also felt the house to be mysteriously stuffy.

The Binkowskis endured the hum for about nine months without relief. They finally had to move out of the house and into a garage to escape it.

Above: this abandoned hut stands in the Oregon Vortex, a spot on the banks of Sardine Creek, Oregon in which the force of gravity intensifies at the center. The pull of the vortex has tilted the hut at an angle.

Right: inside the hut. It is claimed that in spite of the floor, which has a decided slant, a person standing on it inclines to the direction of magnetic north.

suggest. In fact, the space-time warp idea might explain many of the strange phenomena recorded by Fort: the fish, frogs, coal, sand, and rains of blood that have fallen out of clear skies onto the earth. If a space-time warp could transport a Spanish soldier 9000 miles, it might just as easily transport fish from the depths of the sea to the midwestern plains of North America.

Fort mentions in passing a detail that modern researchers may find highly significant: the strange events he records are often accompanied by a failure of electric power in machines. Such an inexplicable power failure occurred in Cairo on April 5, 1923. It is linked by some with the famous "curse of Tutankhamun" because it coincided with the death of the Earl of Carnarvon, the man who sponsored the excavation of Tutankhamun's tomb. The same thing happened in Denver, Colorado, on February 14, 1963: all power failed, and engineers found the failure inexplicable. They were equally baffled when the lights came on again an hour and a half later.

Left: one of the most curious phenomena associated with the Oregon Vortex is the odd change in height that appears to happen within the vortex, particularly marked when two people, one inside and one outside the vortex, compare their heights, as shown in these two photographs. It has been suggested that this might be because photons within the vortex have a uniformly disturbed axis along the magnetic north/magnetic south plane, which would be followed and duplicated by a corresponding aberration in the axis of the atoms. This would result in a change in the physical structure of any object within the field of the mysterious vortex.

Flying saucer enthusiasts point out that similar failures seem to occur in the vicinity of UFOs. For example, on August 17, 1959, the Chief Engineer of the power station in Uberlandia, Minais Gerais, Brazil, saw a large flying object passing over the station. At the same moment, the automatic power switches kicked themselves open. The engineer closed them; they flew open again. The flying object passed over a substation a few miles away, and the keys there flew open in the same way. While the UFO hovered near the station, the keys refused to remain closed. When it flew off, everything functioned normally again.

Ufologists are inclined to believe that the motors of a UFO cause power failures. As far as I know, no one has yet suggested the more interesting hypothesis that UFOs may be associated with space-time warps, and that it is the warp that is to blame.

As the British scientist J. B. S. Haldane once remarked: "The universe is not only stranger than we imagine; it is stranger than we *can* imagine."

3

Devil's Graveyards

It is odd that we should call our planet the Earth. It would be far more reasonable to call it the Sea. Almost *three quarters* of this globe is under water, and if the polar caps melted, about half the remaining land would vanish. We human beings are little better than shipwrecked sailors living on tiny islands. The Pacific Ocean alone is larger than all the land areas of the world, and it is so deep that it could contain the whole land-mass of the moon.

Because we have sailed all over the sea's surface, we believe that we know the sea. This is a fallacy. A mere two percent of the ocean's floor has been charted. At its

An empty ship, drifting aimlessly in a quiet sea: it sounds like the beginning of a thriller, but more than one boarding party has discovered it to be disconcerting reality. A sound ship, obviously abandoned in midocean—why? The insistent question has sometimes never found a convincing answer. Right: crew members of the *Dei Gratia* going to investigate the strange behavior of the *Mary Celeste*, which they found deserted in 1872. It remains one of the unsolved mysteries of the sea, whose deeps hold many enigmas that defy all rational explanation.

"There was no sign of life. The entire lighthouse was empty"

greatest depth, the Pacific Ocean is seven miles deep. As undersea explorer Jacques Cousteau has remarked, the sea is like a bowl of soup, and it gets thicker as you get deeper. It used to be thought that no life could exist at such a depth, but special deep-sea submarines—one of which reached a depth of almost seven miles—have revealed that this is an error. New marine species are always being discovered. In 1938 a fisherman in the Indian Ocean caught a coelacanth, a prehistoric fish that was believed to have died out 60 million years ago. There are reasonable grounds for believing that 100-foot long eels still exist in the ocean. The oceanographer Alain Bombard, making a one-man trip across the Atlantic in a rubber dinghy, was followed by an unknown sea creature he described as "a long, green sausage, about 10 feet long and nine inches or so in diameter. It was not seaweed because it moved and wriggled . . ." The more we learn of the sea, the more obvious it becomes that we have scarcely begun to penetrate its mysteries.

To human beings the most frightening characteristic of the sea is its power to engulf them without trace. I am not speaking of straightforward drowning—the sea has a habit of yielding up its drowned—but of the strange disappearances at sea that are even more numerous and more baffling than those on land.

One of the more curious of the sea's minor enigmas is the mystery of the Eilean Mor lighthouse on the Flannan Islands off the West Coast of Scotland. Ten days before Christmas in 1900, the lighthouse's 140,000 candlepower light was extinguished. Joseph Moore, the relief lighthouse keeper in the Outer Hebrides 17 miles away, could not leave his post to investigate because wild storms of the North Atlantic had battered the coast for a week past.

Among the inhabitants of the Hebrides, the Flannan Islands have the reputation of being haunted. Eilean Mor, the largest of the islands, has a fine green turf that is highly suitable for sheep, and farmers sometimes took their sheep there for fattening. But nothing would persuade them to remain on the island overnight.

On December 26 the storm abated, and the steamer *Hesperus* set out for Eilean Mor with provisions. As the *Hesperus* circled the island, the crew observed that no preparations had been made for their arrival. There were no empty packing cases or mooring ropes on the jetty. A boat was let down, and Joseph Moore was the first ashore. The entrance gate and the main door of the lighthouse were closed. Moore went inside and shouted. There was no reply. The place was cold and empty. The clock on the shelf had stopped. Moore ran back to the jetty for help, afraid that he might find dead men in the lighthouse turret. Two men climbed the stairs with him. But there was no sign of life. The entire lighthouse was empty. In the sleeping quarters the beds were made, and everything was neat and orderly. The wicks of the lanterns had been trimmed, and they had been filled with oil ready to be lit after dark. The last entry on the record slate had been made at 9 a.m. on December 15—the day the light had failed to appear.

At first it looked as if the mystery might be solved. Two of

Below: Alain Bombard, a French oceanographer who made a single-handed journey across the Atlantic in 1952 in a rubber dinghy he called *L'Heretique*. He reported sighting an unidentifiable sea creature that followed his boat.

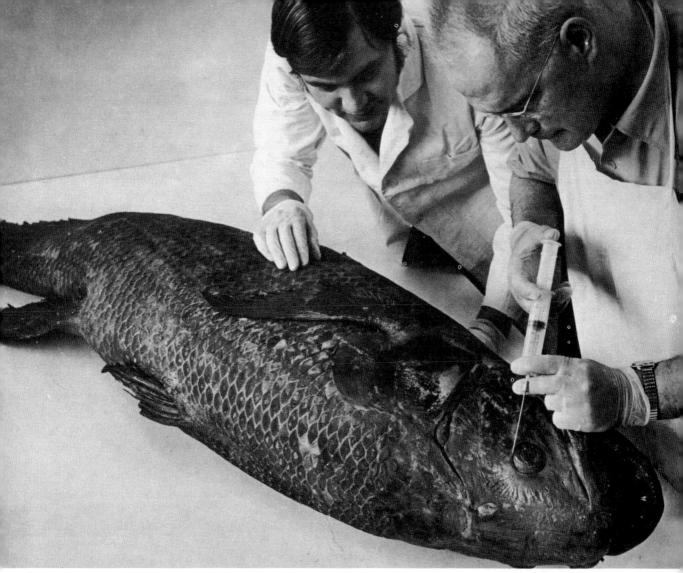

Above: a coelacanth being injected with preservative. The strange fish belongs to a family which until 1938 had been believed to have been extinct for over 60 million years. It is a living fossil. The obvious question presents itself: are there other unsuspected creatures in the depths of the seas?

Left: the human imagination has always been quick to populate the oceans with fantastic beasts. In this 16th-century woodcut, the men are dwarfed by enormous sea serpents and gigantic lobsters.

the three sets of oilskins belonging to the lighthouse keepers were missing. Investigators who landed on the island a few days later found that the west jetty had suffered severe storm damage. On a concrete platform 65 feet above the water stood a crane with ropes trailing from it. These ropes were usually kept in a tool chest, which was placed in a crevice more than a hundred feet above sea level. The chest was found to be missing. The astonishing conclusion was that some tremendous storm, with waves over a hundred feet high, seemed to have battered the island and carried away the chest—draping its ropes over the crane—and swept the three men to their deaths.

For that to have happened was well nigh impossible. To begin with, the day of the 15th had been relatively calm despite a week of storms. If this were not the case, all three oilskins would have been missing, whereas one had been left behind in the lighthouse. Furthermore, experienced lighthouse men would hardly be stupid enough to venture out onto a jetty in a storm.

It seems far more likely that the damage to the jetty had occurred in a storm the previous evening, and that the three men had gone out in calm weather to inspect it. And then what happened? One suggestion that gained wide general acceptance is that one of the three went insane, killed his two companions, and then committed suicide. But no weapons were missing. Hammers, axes, and knives were all untouched in their proper places.

Three men had set out for the west jetty of their lighthouse on a calm day—and vanished. No bodies were ever recovered. No plausible explanation has ever been put forward. Moore, left alone in the lighthouse for two days after landing, believed that he heard men's voices calling to him. Could they have been other than the cry of sea birds? Since 1900 no more disappearances have occurred, and the island has kept its secret.

As we examine some of the classic mysteries of the sea, a pattern begins to emerge. In case after case something frightened the crew into abandoning ship. No one has ever been able to suggest what that something might be.

The case of the Dutch schooner *Hermania* is typical. In 1849 a fishing vessel off the coast of Cornwall in southwest England found the ship drifting. She had been dismasted, evidently by a gale. Men went aboard and found that the schooner's lifeboat was still in its chocks. The property of the crew seemed to be intact, but every living soul aboard the vessel had vanished.

An even stranger mystery was encountered by another British sailing vessel the *Ellen Austin*. In the summer of 1881 the ship was heading for St. John's, Newfoundland. In the mid-Atlantic, the crew sighted a schooner that seemed to be keeping a parallel course. As they came closer they realized that the ship was drifting. A boarding party examined the schooner. Everything seemed to be in order, and there was no sign of a struggle; but the crew was missing. The mate and several crew members from the *Ellen Austin* stayed on board to man the valuable prize, and for some time the two ships continued to sail parallel. Then a storm blew up, driving them

Above: the Eilean Mor lighthouse on the Flannan Islands off the west coast of Scotland. It was from this lighthouse that three keepers vanished so inexplicably on a calm day in 1900.

Left: a keeper tending the great light. The lighthouse is now operated mechanically as an unmanned lighthouse, but until the last few years, three keepers continued to carry out duties.

Below: inside the lighthouse. Most of the furniture is still the same as that used by the vanished men, and the room looks much as it did that day when the three walked out on their mysterious, unexplained errand from which they never returned.

Left: Benjamin Spooner Briggs, the captain of the *Mary Celeste*. Captain Briggs came from a Massachusetts seafaring family, and was a stern and able captain. His ship had been abandoned in haste—but no one knows why.

Right: the *Dei Gratia* sights the *Mary Celeste* drifting about 600 miles west of the Portuguese coast.

apart. When the storm had cleared, the mystery ship seemed to be damaged. The captain saw through his telescope that there was no one on deck. He ordered a boat to be lowered, and went on board. The ship was deserted.

His crew went into a panic. It took the captain a great deal of talking—with offers of reward—to persuade a four-man crew to go aboard the derelict. Again, the two ships proceeded toward Newfoundland. The mystery schooner was faster than the *Ellen Austin*, and soon drew ahead. That didn't bother the captain, however, because he expected to find the ship in St. John's when he arrived. But there was no sign of the schooner in port. It had vanished with the crew members.

In October 1917 the schooner *Zebrina* left Falmouth, England, for France—a fairly short voyage. Two days later, the *Zebrina* was found drifting and deserted with no sign of violence or anything else to indicate why the crew had left. In July 1941 the Portuguese lugger *Islandia* sighted the French cutter *Belle Isle* near the Gulf of Lyon. The sails of the cutter were set and undamaged. There was no one aboard, and no clue to the disappearance of the sailors was found. All these cases seem to have the same strange element in common—the mysterious something that caused panic, and left no clue behind.

The chief problem in most of these cases is lack of adequate documentation, which leads the critical reader to suspect the

accuracy of most popular accounts. In at least two classic cases, however, we have accurate and detailed documentation. These are the mysteries of the *Mary Celeste* and the *Joyita*.

From the beginning, the American vessel *Mary Celeste* was an unlucky ship. Her first captain died a few days after taking command. On her first voyage she damaged her hull. In the Straits of Dover she collided with a brig and sank it. In 1867, only six years after her launching, she grounded on Cape Breton Island, Nova Scotia, and was assumed to be a write-off. A man who salvaged her went bankrupt.

In the autumn of 1872, with this history behind her, the *Mary Celeste* set out from New York with a cargo of commercial alcohol. Captain Benjamin Briggs had his wife and two-year-old daughter on board, and there was a crew of seven. The *Mary Celeste* sailed for the Italian port of Genoa on November 5. Ten days later, the British ship *Dei Gratia* also left New York bound for Gibraltar. Her captain was David Moorhouse.

On the afternoon of December 5, 1872 the *Dei Gratia* sighted the *Mary Celeste* in the North Atlantic, midway between the Azores and the coast of Portugal. She was obviously drifting. A boarding party found her deserted. The lifeboat was missing, indicating that the crew had abandoned ship in some kind of danger. But there was nothing noticeably wrong with

Lost Planes Over the Sargasso Sea

How can a plane with all its crew and passengers disappear without a trace? No bodies ever found. Not a piece of wreckage ever recovered. A total mystery.

This happened to two British airliners about three years after the end of World War II. The first to vanish was the *Star Ariel* on January 17, 1949. It was crossing the sinister waters of the Sargasso Sea, that mysterious region of the Atlantic Ocean which itself is a part of the equally mysterious Bermuda Triangle. Above these strange waters of floating seaweed the plane vanished.

A large-scale sea and air rescue attempt was put into operation. Destroyers searched thoroughly on the sea. Seven U.S. Coast Guard and naval aircraft searched from the sky, crossing and recrossing the entire area in close formation. Neither the ships nor the planes found anything at all.

There was another odd occurrence in connection with *Star Ariel*, however. A British commercial plane and an American bomber reported sighting a strange light and a floating object that reflected the moonlight in the sea about 300 miles south of Bermuda. It was in the very same area that *Star Ariel* had disappeared.

Thirteen days later on January 30, 1949 the airliner *Star Tiger* vanished in the same region and in the same way as *Star Ariel*. Again all searches proved fruitless, and neither bodies nor parts of the plane turned up.

A government committee in Great Britain investigated the strange events. The committee even went to the length of taking apart a plane like the two that had vanished in order to study it in detail.

Like every other investigation, this one found no clues.

the vessel. There were a few feet of water in the hold, but the ship's pumps proved to be working perfectly, and this was soon pumped out. The condition of the crew's quarters indicated that the ship had been abandoned in extreme haste. In the hold a few barrels of the commercial alcohol had broken open, and one was empty. The hatch of the hold was found on deck.

With some difficulty a skeleton crew sailed the *Mary Celeste* to Gibraltar, arriving on December 13. Right from the start they met with hostility. The British authorities in Gibraltar suspected that the men of the *Dei Gratia* were in collusion with the crew of the *Mary Celeste* to claim salvage money. The *Mary Celeste* was searched, and on December 18 an inquiry was heard in the Vice-Admiralty Court of Gibraltar. The Queen's Advocate, Solly Flood, who cross-examined the witnesses, concluded that there had been a mutiny aboard the *Mary Celeste*, and that the crew had killed the captain and his family. Searchers had found a cutlass under the captain's bed, and Flood maintained that certain stains on it were blood. The hull of the ship appeared to have been damaged, and Flood believed that the mutineers did this to make it look as if the vessel had struck rocks. The United States consul in Gibraltar disagreed hotly with this view. He insisted that there were no signs whatever of violence or mutiny aboard the *Mary Celeste*, and that the damage to the hull was natural.

The crew of the *Dei Gratia* was finally awarded £1700 salvage money—a mere fraction of the ship's value. And so the whole incident was forgotten—for 11 years. At that time an impecunious young doctor with ambitions to become an author wrote a story based on the affair. Entitled *J. Habakuk Jephson's Statement*, the story appeared anonymously in *The Cornhill Magazine* in January 1884 with the ship's name changed to the *Marie Celeste*. The story claimed that she had been taken over as part of what would now be called a Black Power plot. It also claimed that the vessel's lifeboat was still on board when she was found. When the identity of the author became known, he found himself launched on the road to fame.

The author was Arthur Conan Doyle, and his fictional version of the *Mary Celeste* mystery started a flood of books and articles on the subject. Most of them were speculation or pure fiction, and none of these accounts succeeded in throwing any light on the reasons for the ship's abandonment. One of the few plausible suggestions is that some of the alcohol on board exploded—which could account for the hatch being on the deck—and the captain decided that they should all climb into one lifeboat to be towed behind the *Mary Celeste*. At some point, the tow broke and everyone drowned. The only objection to this explanation is that there was no sign of an explosion in the hold.

The *Joyita* is often referred to as the *Mary Celeste* of the Pacific. It was a twin-screw ship that met with disaster in October 1955 some time after leaving Apia in Western Samoa. It was headed for Fakaofo in the Tokelau Islands, a mere 270 miles to the north. On November 10, more than a month after she had set out, the *Joyita* was found abandoned and half-foundering. But the ship was cork-lined, and therefore practic-

Above: the *Joyita* as it was found by a Fiji ship in 1955 after an air search. The boat was half foundering, and there was not a soul aboard. Again, like the *Mary Celeste*, there is no certain explanation of why the boat was suddenly abandoned. Left: Captain Thomas "Dusty" Miller and his wife. Less than two weeks after the boat was found, Mrs. Miller sued for divorce on the grounds of desertion. Miller is now presumed to be dead. Below left: the waterlogged *Joyita*, towed into a lagoon on the Fijian island of Vanua Levu. Although half swamped, the boat, which was cork-lined, was still afloat, and in fact was almost unsinkable for all practical purposes. The mystery still remains: why did the captain, who knew she would not sink, abandon her?

ally unsinkable. The captain, Dusty Miller, had known that perfectly well—in fact, he had often boasted of it. His officers knew it too. So why had they abandoned ship?

Stranger still, there were signs that two men had stayed aboard. An awning had been erected either to catch water or to keep off the sun. Where had these men gone?

There could be no doubt whatever that the *Joyita* had been in trouble. In fact, only one of the two engines was working, and the radio was defective. She was hardly seaworthy.

The ship was taken to Suva, Fiji where she was dry-docked and pumped out. The basic cause of the trouble was soon apparent. A pipe under the boiler room floor had broken and flooded the vessel. Blood-stained bandages were found. This suggested that someone had been injured fairly seriously—probably the captain himself, since he would otherwise not have permitted the crew to abandon ship. It therefore seemed possible to reconstruct the tragedy. Somewhere out at sea, the

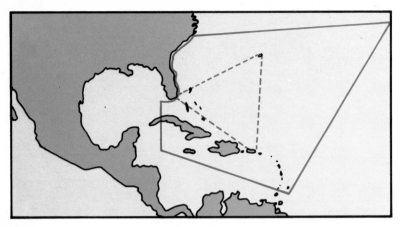

Left: the Bermuda Triangle, an area in the Atlantic Ocean in which many disappearances of ships and aircraft have occurred. There is a great difference of opinion among investigators as to the exact area of the Triangle: the inner dotted line shows the traditional area, and the red continuous line includes areas that various authors have considered as being part of it.

Above: Avenger torpedo bombers of the kind that vanished on a routine training flight off the east coast of Florida in 1955. Five planes were first involved.

Right: a Martin Mariner seaplane. With 13 crewmen aboard, a similar Martin Mariner took off as part of the search operation. Like the five planes it was hunting, it vanished completely, and nothing has ever been found of either the plane or its unfortunate crew.

Joyita's engine stopped. The pipe burst and caused flooding. Captain Miller had somehow been badly injured, perhaps by being thrown from the bridge by a sudden listing. The crew and passengers had taken to the boats, and had perished at sea. Miller had remained on board, probably with a devoted attendant to look after him.

And then . . . what? At this point, we once again meet with a mystery. Did some new panic cause the captain and his companion to abandon ship? That is unlikely, since Miller knew that his ship was unsinkable. Even if the captain had died of his wound and was thrown overboard, surely his companion would have remained. One theory is that the drifting vessel encountered a pirate ship, and that Miller and his companion were murdered. It is true that some of the cargo was missing; but it seems likely that this was thrown overboard in the original panic to lighten the ship. In the two decades since it met disaster, the *Joyita* has joined the *Mary Celeste* as one of the unsolved mysteries of the sea. At this stage, it seems unlikely that the truth will ever come to light.

The cases described so far have occurred in many different parts of the world, but there are two small areas that have been responsible for more disappearances than the rest of the world put together. They are know as the "Bermuda Triangle" and the "Devil's Sea." One lies in the Atlantic off the east coast of the United States, the other in the Pacific southeast of Japan. Both have acquired a singularly evil reputation.

The term "Bermuda Triangle" was coined by the author of a book on sea mysteries, Vincent Gaddis, who also called it the "Triangle of Death." Gaddis was among the first to notice the incredible number of disappearances of ships and aircraft in this relatively small area off the coast of Florida. Well over a hundred such disappearances have been recorded, with the loss of more than a thousand lives. Most of these mysteries have occurred since 1945, and the disappearances have been total. Not a single body nor a fragment of wreckage from the vanished craft has ever been recovered.

A typical disappearance took place on January 8, 1962. A big United States Air Force Boeing Stratotanker took off from Langley, Virginia, and flew east for the Azores. Shortly afterward the control tower received weak radio signals from the plane. When these ceased, the wide-scale search was launched. But no trace of the aircraft was ever found.

The long saga of disappearances in the Triangle begins in the year 1609. A ship called the *Sea Venture*, bearing English settlers to Virginia, was shipwrecked off the island of Bermuda. On September 1, the longboat of the wrecked vessel set out on the 500-mile voyage to the coast of the United States to bring help. With a fair wind in its sail, it passed beyond the horizon— and was never seen again.

In 1750 five Spanish treasure ships were caught in storms off Cape Hatteras. Three of them vanished completely, and no wreckage was found.

In 1800 two United States Navy ships vanished in the area. In his book on the Bermuda Triangle, Charles Berlitz lists 12 more cases of major vessels that have disappeared in the

Escape From Oblivion

In November 1964 Chuck Wakely, a pilot for a charter flight airline, had a narrow escape from being swallowed up by the unknown forces of the Bermuda Triangle. At the time of his frightening experience, he knew nothing about the perils of that area.

Wakely's brush with fate occurred on a return solo flight from Nassau to Miami. He climbed to 8000 feet, leveled off, and settled back for a routine run. Then he noticed a faint glow on the wings of his plane. He put it down to an optical illusion created by the cockpit lights through the tinted windows.

After about five minutes, however, the glow increased so much that Wakely found it hard to read his instruments. Soon he had to operate the craft manually because none of the electronic equipment was in working order.

He noticed that the wings glowed bluish-green and looked fuzzy. At that point he was in such operating difficulties that he had to let go of the controls and let the plane take its head. The glow became blinding, but then began to fade.

As soon as the glow had died down, the instruments began to work properly again. Wakely was able to make a normal landing at his destination.

He was one of the lucky ones.

Triangle, and no less than seven cases of ships found drifting, like the *Mary Celeste*, abandoned but basically undamaged. His list begins with the *Rosalie*, a large French vessel found abandoned in 1840 with sails set and cargo intact, and ends with the total disappearance on March 23, 1973 of the 20,000 ton freighter *Anita*.

The disappearance of planes in the Triangle area began on December 5, 1945, when five United States Navy aircraft vanished on a routine training flight. Each plane should have been manned by an officer pilot and two crew members, but one of the crew members had a premonition of disaster and stayed away. The planes were Avenger torpedo bombers, and each had enough fuel for more than a thousand miles. Their projected flight was less than 500 miles. They took off from their base at Fort Lauderdale, Florida, at 2 p.m. At about 3:15 p.m., the control tower received a strange message from the flight leader. He reported that the planes seemed to be off course, and he could not see land. Asked to state his position, he said he didn't know. Clearly the aircrafts' compasses and navigation gear were not functioning. This was confirmed shortly afterward when control overheard conversations between the planes in which crew members referred to the instruments in all the planes as "going crazy." Each registered a different reading, they said. Meanwhile, heavy static had begun to obscure communications. The planes seemed unable to hear the base transmitter, and it became increasingly difficult for control to hear them. The last barely audible message from the planes was received at 4 p.m. It said again that the pilots could not be sure where they were.

Rescue planes were dispatched among which was a twin-engined Martin Mariner with a crew of 13. Shortly after takeoff, base also lost contact with the Martin Mariner. Like the five planes it sought, it was never heard from again. In spite of an intensive search involving over 300 planes and many hundreds of sailing vessels, no trace of the six missing aircraft was ever found.

In his book Charles Berlitz lists 14 more planes that have disappeared in the Triangle area since 1945. In case after case, the same phrase recurs: "lost radio contact."

Berlitz was by no means the first person to write about the Bermuda Triangle, but he was the first to investigate reports of people who had narrowly escaped its strange perils. Captain Don Henry, owner of a salvage company in Florida, described how, in 1966, he was aboard a tug towing an empty petroleum nitrate barge. The weather was clear and calm. Suddenly the tug's compass began to spin clockwise. The sea became turbulent. "We couldn't see where the horizon was—the water, sky, and horizon all blended together," Captain Henry recalled. All electrical apparatus stopped working. The generators continued to run, but there was no electricity. The barge had vanished beneath a cloud of fog. Henry signaled full speed ahead, but had the feeling that something was holding them back. Then suddenly the tug pulled free. For a few minutes the barge remained hidden in a dense fog—although there was no fog anywhere else—but the tug gradually towed it out. The

Top: a poster offering a reward for any information about the missing yacht *Saba Bank*, one of the many boats that have vanished in the Bermuda Triangle area.

Above: the *Sulphur Queen*, a tanker that left the port of Beaumont, Texas, on the morning of February 2, 1963. A perfectly normal radio message was received from the ship the next day, but after that nothing more was ever heard of her.

Above: sister ship of the *Good News*, the tug that escaped from a strange experience in the Triangle in 1966. The tug, pulling a barge, lost all electrical power, and the compass began spinning as a sudden fog came down. The captain, feeling that something was pulling both tug and barge backward, desperately rammed the throttles full ahead, and managed at last to move out of the fog. Back in the calm sea, both vessels moved on without any difficulty.

Right: three days after the last radio message, rescue planes and cutters took part in an extensive search, which managed to come up with the few bits of equipment pictured—a life jacket, a life belt, and a man's shirt. It was all that has ever been found of the *Sulphur Queen* and the 39 men that had sailed in her. No oil spots, no drifting boats, no other pieces of the missing ship. It was as if the 7240-ton tanker had purely and simply dissolved.

Above: Charles Berlitz, who has written a best selling account of the peculiarities of the Bermuda Triangle. The grandson of the man who founded the Berlitz language schools, he is an accomplished linguistic expert himself.

tug's generators began to work normally again, but all the batteries were dead, and several flashlight batteries had to be thrown away.

A pilot, Chuck Wakeley, described how he was flying from Nassau to Fort Lauderdale in 1964 when the wings of his aircraft began to glow until the whole plane became luminous. The electric automatic pilot immediately went wrong, and all other electrical instruments cut out or behaved erratically. Wakeley tried to operate the plane manually, but the glow from the aircraft was blinding. He was forced to let the plane fly where it would. After five terrifying minutes, the glow began to fade slowly, and the instruments started to work normally.

In April 1963 the crew of a Boeing 707 observed what looked like an atomic explosion in the sea. They saw the water rise up into a great mound, half a mile wide. The pilot later checked with the coast guard and meteorological agencies to find out if there had been an earthquake in the area, but he was told that no unusual occurrences had been reported.

The baffling element in most of these accounts is not the strange behavior of the compasses, but the loss of electric power. Compasses behave strangely if brought close to a large magnet or mass of iron ore, and there could well be some vast iron deposit under the seabed in the Triangle area. But there is no way known to science of draining a battery of its charge, or preventing a generator from producing electricity—if there were, it would be an invaluable weapon of war. Yet the force that operates in the area of the Bermuda Triangle seems to interfere with electrical circuits.

The evidence about sea disappearances, like those on land, appears to tie in with the notion of some disturbance of the gravitational field—an "antigravity warp"—in which the conventional laws of gravity do not operate in accustomed ways. However, such speculation only serves to emphasize how little we really know about gravity, and that we have no way of judging how it might be affected by local conditions. All we can say is that, *if* there is such a thing as an antigravity warp, the local conditions in the Bermuda Triangle would certainly appear to be an example of it.

The same observation may well apply to the "Devil's Sea"—an area in the Pacific 800 miles southeast of Japan between Iwo Jima and Marcus Island. Perhaps because this area is so far from the coast of Japan, its mysteries have never aroused the same excitement as those of the Bermuda Triangle. There had been occasional disappearances of ships and aircraft in the area over a long period; but between 1950 and 1954 no less than nine ships disappeared without trace. The Japanese government then became concerned, and declared it a danger zone. In 1955 the government sponsored an expedition to the area, and a group of scientists set sail aboard the *Kaiyo Maru No. 5*. The *Kaiyo Maru* itself vanished.

Ivan T. Sanderson, an avid collector of strange incidents, tried marking the Bermuda Triangle and the Devil's Sea on a map. He observed that the two areas lie in roughly the same latitude—between 30° and 40° north of the Equator—and are

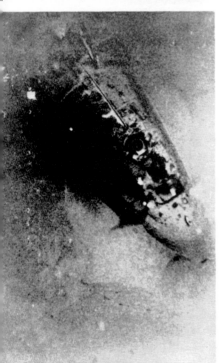

Above: among the craft that have encountered disaster from unknown causes was the submarine *U.S.S. Scorpion*, pictured at the launching ceremonies in 1959. It vanished in May 1968.

Left: the first photograph released by the Navy of the sunken *Scorpion*. It was located in October 1968 at a depth of just under two miles underwater, 400 miles southwest of the Azores.

Below: the 20,000-ton Norwegian cargo ship the *Anita*, which was another ship to disappear mysteriously in the Triangle.

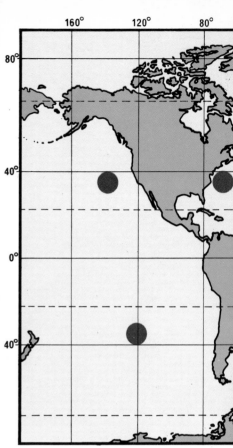

Above: Ivan Sanderson, naturalist and writer, who investigated many unexplained phenomena. He made the suggestion that the Bermuda Triangle was just one of the areas of ocean known as "devil's graveyards," more notorious because within its area are found very heavily traveled sea lanes.

approximately the same size. Other observations of areas known as "devil's graveyards" led Sanderson to conclude that there are 12 such zones lying symmetrically around the world. Two of these are the North and South poles. Others lie neatly at intervals of 72° around the globe, and are centered at 36° north and south latitudes. Sanderson suggests that the Bermuda Triangle is the most notorious because it happens to be one of the busiest areas of the world. Apart from the Poles, only two of the devil's graveyards lie on land—one in the area of the Sahara desert, the other in the mountainous region of northwestern India.

Sanderson noted that most of the suspect areas lie in parts of the ocean where warm and cold currents collide, and that these areas are "nodal points" where surface and subsurface currents turn in different directions. His suggestion is that the powerful sweeping movement of subsurface tidal currents, influenced by variations in temperature, causes magnetic vortices that are the root of the trouble. There is no evidence, however, that the collision of ocean currents produces changes in the earth's magnetism. There is no reason why it should. Nor does Sanderson's theory apply to the land areas—the Sahara, northern India, the Poles. If "magnetic vortices" provide the answer isn't it more likely that these are nodal points in the earth's field of power?

It must be acknowledged that Sanderson has provided the basis for an interesting theory. Even his suggestion, however, fails to explain why so many ships have been found abandoned, with no clue as to what caused the crew to leave in panic.

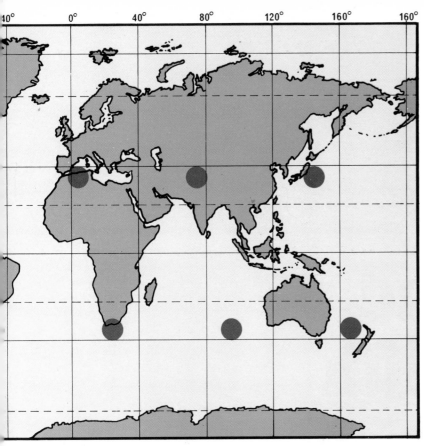

Left: a map showing Sanderson's placing of the twelve "devil's graveyards." Two, the North and South poles, are not shown. Each is centered at 36° north and south of the Equator, producing five in the Northern Hemisphere and five in the Southern, plus the poles. Only two fall in land areas.

Below: the *Kaiyo Maru 5*, which in 1955 vanished in the Devil's Sea—another mystery area located in the Pacific Ocean southeast of Japan. The ship was on an investigatory expedition sponsored by the Japanese government when it disappeared, scientists and all.

4

The Road to the Fifth Dimension

The late T. C. Lethbridge was an enthusiastic exponent of the technique of *radiesthesia*. I use this term in its sense of the knack of finding things with the aid of a pendulum or dowsing rod. In a book called *Ghost and Divining Rod*, Lethbridge explains how he carried out a simple experiment in radiesthesia. He started by carving a one-inch ball out of a piece of hazel wood and threading the ball on a piece of string precisely 22 inches long. He then went into the courtyard of his home—part of which had been built in the 14th century—and walked around slowly, holding the pendulum by its string. After a short time, the

"Some very powerful force was apparently at work"

back-and-forth swing of the pendulum changed to a circular motion. Lethbridge then took a spade, and proceeded to dig cautiously at the point the motion had changed. Just under the turf he found a piece of 17th-century pottery, and six inches lower a piece of 17th-century Rhineland stoneware. But this was not what he was looking for. Twenty-two inches is the length at which the pendulum should be able to locate silver. Lethbridge held his pendulum over the heap of earth from the hole. It swung in a circle. He searched carefully through the heap of earth, but failed to find the expected silver. Finally, as he was filling the hole, he found another piece of old stoneware. He held the pendulum over it, and the pendulum swung with a violent circular movement. Then he remembered: old stoneware is glazed with lead salts, and lead is on the same "wavelength" as silver. The mystery was explained.

Any reader who is inclined to dismiss this as a typical crank theory should first of all try dowsing—an art that is thousands of years old. Take any kind of bead or bob and thread it on the end of a long piece of string. Now take a ruler, and measure off precisely 24 inches on the string. Ask any male of your acquaintance to lie down on the floor, and hold the pendulum over him. Start the pendulum swinging gently to and fro. After a few moments, this arc swing will change to a circular motion. If you hold the pendulum over a female, nothing will happen—the pendulum will continue to swing back and forth. However, if you increase the length of the string to 29 inches, the pendulum will react over women, and will show no reaction for men. This is because 29 inches is the so-called "female length." According to diviners, each substance has its own wavelength. Twenty-four inches will locate diamonds and males. Twenty-nine inches will locate gold, females, and anything colored yellow.

The behavior of a ball on the end of a piece of string may seem a far cry from the mysterious electrical or magnetic fields that can cause a ship's compass to spin wildly. However, it is significant that dowsers have insisted on the existence of such fields for centuries. Indeed, the dowser's ability to locate water, minerals, and other substances underground may be due to picking up the activity of these fields.

Lethbridge tells an interesting story about visiting an ancient stone circle called the Merry Maidens near Penzance, England. This circle is believed to date from the same time as Stonehenge, about 1500 B.C. Presumably it served some religious purpose, but nobody knows what. Lethbridge tried his pendulum close to one of the stones, setting it at 30 inches. This is the length that diviners use for testing the age of ancient monuments. As he held the pendulum, Lethbridge rested his free hand on the stone megalith. Almost as soon as the pendulum started to swing, the hand resting on the stone received a tingling sensation like an electric shock, and the pendulum began to circle so strongly that it was almost horizontal to the ground. Some very powerful force was apparently at work.

I have myself experienced the mysterious force at the Merry Maidens when dowsing with a friend who is interested in the subject. Although I had only tried dowsing once before—without success—on this occasion I obtained a powerful reaction. I

Left: an engraving showing the various traditional ways of holding the dowsing rod. Most people are usually familiar with dowsing for water, but experienced dowsers claim they can locate any material lying underground.

Left: the Merry Maidens, where both Lethbridge and the author reported that their dowsing efforts put them in contact with a powerful and mysterious force.

Below: the author dowsing at the Merry Maidens, an ancient stone circle in the south of England.

Why Churches Were Built Crooked

The altar in most Christian churches is placed at the east end of the building. This is a tradition based on the idea that facing the direction of the sunrise symbolizes turning toward spiritual light.

This tradition, oddly enough, may account for the fact that the nave and chancel of many of the old churches in Great Britain lie at an angle to each other rather than in a straight line. In Oxfordshire alone, for example, there are 81 churches with crooked chancels, which is the part of the building housing the altar. Why were these and many other chancels throughout the rest of the country built at an angle?

The Reverend Hugh Benson of Plymouth, England thinks it is because the churches were meant to face sunrise on the exact festival day of their particular patron saint.

According to his letter-to-the-editor of *The Times* of London in 1975, Reverend Benson has studied this matter over a period of years, and has examined nearly a thousand churches. After making careful calculations, he became convinced that a great many churches had in fact faced sunrise on their saint's day at the time they were built. There were only about half a dozen exceptions to this finding in the whole of his survey.

"Now it follows," he says, "that a church built in honor of St. Mary, for example, and facing sunrise on March 25, would after a century or so, owing to the Julian calendar, be found to be facing too far south. If then a new chancel was built, it would be set out to face the new sunrise position. . . The crookedness of the chancel, far from being due to carelessness, is due to a most scrupulous care."

was using a dowsing rod, a common alternative to the pendulum, made of two thin springy strips of whalebone tied together at one end. As I walked toward the center of the stone circle, holding the rod as directed by my friend, the rod began to push upward until it was pointing toward the sky. (For some people a dowsing rod reacts by pointing upward, for others it dips downward.)

I wondered if the strain on my fingers was causing the rod to point upward. I tried the experiment of making it dip down instead. It refused. I tried holding it so tight that it could not move. It was impossible. As I passed over the same spot, it twisted up so strongly that I could not hold it still.

The power was particularly strong in the center of the circle. I asked my friend what this meant, and he said he did not know. It could mean water, but this was unlikely because we kept getting the same reaction all around the stone circle at a point just beyond the outer perimeter.

I do not know what this force is. All I can say, with complete confidence, is that it exists. It could be some form of magnetism in the earth. Perhaps the ancient Britons located this "magnetic circle" with dowsing rods and deliberately built their religious monument there. Lethbridge believed that these "earth forces" can be increased and intensified by generations of worship and religious sacrifice. This could explain why his hand began to tingle when he placed it on the stone.

The Merry Maidens is discussed by John Michell in his book *The Old Stones of Lands End*. Michell points out that this whole area is covered with *leys*—the "old straight tracks" or lines first observed by Alfred Watkins. The Merry Maidens is the focus of such a system of leys. You can draw neat straight lines from its center through other local landmarks, like ancient *barrows* (prehistoric burial mounds) and other standing stones. Michell has suggested that leys are identical with the ancient Chinese dragon paths. If this is so, it seems just conceivable that when the dowsing rods twisted in my hands, I was experiencing the magnetic force of the dragon paths, and that the power which made the rods twist so violently at the center of the circle springs from the union of several dragon paths at this point.

One of the first persons to notice the alignment of ancient sites in the area of the Merry Maidens was the eminent British astronomer Sir Norman J. Lockyer, who wrote a book on Stonehenge and other British stone circles in the early years of this century. Lockyer's theory was that such monuments were not merely religious centers, but also sophisticated astronomical observatories. When certain stars came into alignment with a particular stone and the top of a burial mound, Lockyer suggested, the ancient priests would know that it was time for a certain religious ceremony or sacrifice.

When Lockyer first published his theory, it aroused skepticism and even downright hostility among scientists. Many objected that ancient cultures lacked the knowledge to construct anything so complicated. In recent years, however, Lockyer's theory has been revived by scientists like Alexander Thom, Professor of Engineering Science at Oxford University, and Gerald Hawkins, Professor of Astronomy at Boston

Left: the curious circle of the Callanish standing stones on the Isle of Lewis, one of the Outer Hebrides west of Scotland. It was apparently built as a kind of sacred astronomical observatory.

Above: Sir Norman Lockyer, the brilliant English astronomer who died in 1920. In his book about Stonehenge and other stone monuments, published in 1906, he considered the ancient monoliths from an astronomical standpoint —perhaps because astronomy has been important to human culture since earliest recorded times.

Right: the strange stone avenues of Carnac, a megalithic monument in Brittany, France. The purpose of these curious lines of stones —some 20 feet high and measuring 20 to 30 feet in diameter—has been suggested as everything from an astronomical observatory to landing signals for prehistoric visitors from outer space.

Left: the small cove of Ladram Bay on the south coast of Devon, England. It was on this beach in 1962 that both Lethbridge and his wife, out collecting seaweed, were gripped with an irrational sense of depression and fear. He gave the name of "ghoul" to the queer sensation, and went on to speculate that the sense of evil was in fact a kind of recording of the past, caught and imprinted somehow by water.

Above: Lethbridge and his wife in the course of an investigation.

Left: the Sussex Ghost Hunters, a group of English investigators who attempt to verify the presence of ghosts using scientific techniques. Here they are using a pendulum to check for the ghostly presence that had been alleged to exist in the room.

University. As a result of their research, an increasing number of scientists now accept that Stonehenge, the Merry Maidens, and other megalithic monuments like Carnac in northwest France, were designed as astronomical observatories. Even more amazing was the discovery that astronomical measurements made in these observatories were of incredible accuracy. For example, the moon deviates from its regular course by an almost imperceptible amount—0.9 degrees over a long period. Yet when Hawkins and Thom studied the methods of observation used by the builders of Stonehenge and Callanish (a stone circle in the Outer Hebrides), they discovered that this minute deviation of 0.9 degrees had been recognized more than 3000 years ago. It was not discovered by modern astronomers until the 16th century.

Why should prehistoric man want to observe the heavens so minutely? Why should he want to construct an observatory that was also a church? There can be no doubt that sites such as Stonehenge were used for religious observances. Of course, many modern churches are constructed so that the window behind the altar catches the light of the rising sun; but that is purely a question of dramatic effect. It would certainly cause comment if we installed computers behind the altars of our cathedrals, or used the towers to house astronomical telescopes.

The explanation almost certainly lies in the ancient science of astrology. It seems likely that the builders of Stonehenge and other such temples believed that there were certain times of the year when the stars were propitious for the performance of religious rites, and when the hidden forces of the earth could be harnessed for religious purposes. Our ancestors observed that the tides are affected by the moon, and that certain people become "lunatics" at the time of the full moon. They believed that the hidden forces that populate the earth also rise and fall according to the movements of the heavenly bodies. For example, an eclipse of the moon affects the level of the earth's magnetism, and this may have been why the prehistoric astronomers attached particular importance to the prediction of eclipses. The very sacredness of a sacred place like Stonehenge would reach a maximum intensity at periods when the influence of the heavenly bodies on the earth's forces were strongest. These would be the obvious times for major religious rites.

The moon, being closer to the earth, has a greater influence on magnetic forces such as tides. Therefore we might expect the megaliths to be more concerned with the observation of the moon than of the stars. This, according to Professor Hawkins, is precisely the case.

Lethbridge, who was a professional ethnologist and archeologist as well as a dowser, became convinced that there are at least three distinct varieties of magnetic fields—one associated with water, one with mountains, and one with deserts and other open spaces. The theory of the "water fields"—or "naiad fields," as he prefers to call them—came about as a result of a curious experience in Ladram Bay in 1962. Lethbridge and his wife had driven down to the bay, which is little more than a small cove, to collect seaweed for an asparagus bed. "As I stepped onto the beach," says Lethbridge, "I passed into a kind

Ghosts in Love

Experiments with dowsing led the British ethnologist T. C. Lethbridge to believe strongly in magnetic fields, or fields of force, as a possible explanation of ghosts. He tells this story about one ghost he saw.

According to Lethbridge, he was standing on a hill above a mill. A little stream ran nearby, vanishing into the slope of the hill. Below him, about 60 yards away, a woman stood near the mill. Her clothes were about 40 years out of date. On investigation he discovered that no one remotely resembling the woman he had seen had been near the mill at the time. He had seen a ghost.

Lethbridge explained this by his field-of-force theory. Someone, he said, had once been on the hill, and had seen the figure he had seen. The sight caused such a strong emotion in the viewer "that a picture of her was impressed in the electromagnetic field of the streamlet." Lethbridge had caught sight of the original impression.

Later Lethbridge learned that the mill owner had seen a ghost on the hill. It was a man, dressed in the fashion of 40 years ago. It was obvious to Lethbridge that his ghost and the mill owner's ghost had, when alive, been happy to see each other. Each had impressed a picture of the other on the one field of force.

of blanket, or fog, of depression and, I think, fear." After ten minutes his wife hurried up, saying, "There's something frightful here. Let's go home."

That evening Mrs. Lethbridge called her mother and mentioned the visit to Ladram Bay, whereupon her mother commented that she had once been to the cove and had experienced a feeling of depression there. On his next visit to the bay a week later, Lethbridge again noticed the same "bank of depression" in precisely the same place. It was where a small stream ran into the shingle. At the other end of the beach, his wife pointed out the rock where, the previous week, the feeling of depression had driven her away. The rock lay between two little streams that trickled down the cliff face onto the beach. Lethbridge stood by the rock, and the feeling of depression there was so overwhelming that it made him feel giddy. The couple then climbed to the cliff top overlooking the bay. Mrs. Lethbridge went to look at a point on the edge of the cliff, and experienced a feeling as if someone or something were urging her to jump.

Some people might have concluded that the beach was haunted by a suicide. But Lethbridge had had similar experiences before—for example, seeing the ghost of a woman near his home three years earlier. He had made the interesting observation that, at the time when he saw the ghost, he was standing beside a stream, and that the ghost appeared at a point where the stream vanished underground. Could the ghost have been some kind of *recording* associated with water? But if it was a recording, what was the "tape" on which it was recorded? As a dowser who already accepted that water had its own peculiar field, Lethbridge concluded that the water field was responsible. After the experience at Ladram Bay, Lethbridge noted that conditions there were somewhat similar. The sensations of depression and fear had occurred in the area of streams that trickled into the shingle, and the weather had been damp and muggy at the time. Lethbridge's conclusion was that the field of water can somehow record human emotions, thoughts, and even images, and that the ghost of Ladram beach was actually a recording, rendered more perceptible by the damp weather. Lethbridge calls these recordings "ghouls." Others have called them "thought fields."

Lethbridge's theory could be the key to a mysterious death that occurred in England in 1939. On the morning of May 10 searchers found the body of Harry Dean lying at the foot of a boulder in an abandoned quarry on the slopes of Bredon Hill, Gloucestershire. On the previous evening, Dean had gone for a stroll on Bredon Hill. When he failed to return home his wife notified the police.

The strange thing was that there was no obvious cause for death. Since Dean was lying on the floor of the quarry, the likeliest explanation was that he had fallen from the surrounding cliff some 50 feet above; but the body was unbruised. A post mortem examination revealed the astonishing fact that he had been strangled by his own tie. The coroner concluded that Dean had climbed the three-foot-high boulder at whose foot he was found, and that he had slipped and displaced the cartilage of his leg. He had fainted and been choked by his tie.

There was never any suggestion that Dean had been the victim of foul play. Nothing was missing from his pockets, and there were no signs of a struggle. Yet it seemed extraordinary that an accidental fall from a boulder only three feet high could result in a man's death.

The sheer improbability of the coroner's explanation led local author Harold Wilkins to undertake his own investigation. He deliberately waited a whole year until May 1940 so that conditions would be as similar as possible to those at the time of Harry Dean's death. He then visited the quarry with his brother. The first thing Wilkins noticed about Death Quarry was that its floor had evidently been leveled many centuries before the site's use as a quarry, which archeologists have dated as around 750 B.C. On this flat floor at the four points of the compass, Wilkins noticed four weathered boulders. Dean's body had been found by the one at the south end.

Wilkins and his brother made their way out of the quarry, up a grass-embanked causeway with unopened Stone Age barrows, past two ancient obelisks known as the "King and Queen stones," to the Iron Age fort on the top of Bredon Hill. This fort dates from the 5th century B.C., and excavations have uncovered the skeletons of 50 men who had died in battle and had been mutilated by the enemy. Their heads, arms, and legs had been chopped off. In one corner of the fort stands a strange cracked stone known as the Bambury Stone. Archeological evidence suggests that this was once an object of religious worship, perhaps an altar for sacrificial victims. Wilkins clambered onto the Bambury Stone to be photographed by his brother. As he did so, both men heard a sudden thud, as if a heavy object had fallen on the grass above them. Intrigued and puzzled, they searched the ground. It was a still, clear day, but they were unable to find anything that could account for the noise. "Something eerie and sinister had demonstrated its presence and its objection to the photographing of this weird stone," says Wilkins. He goes on to suggest that Harry Dean was strangled by some "unseen entity" as he stood at the foot of the boulder. Wilkins points out that Bredon Hill forms a rough quadrilateral with other hills. In another corner stands Long Compton Hill with its circle of megaliths known as the Rollright Stones, used as the site of Witches' Sabbaths in the Middle Ages. In another corner of the quadrilateral is Meon Hill, again associated with black magic and witchcraft, and also with the apparition of a black dog. Wilkins suggests that such sites are imbued with dark and violent forces associated with pagan religious rites. Significantly, the priests of ancient Britain held one of their most important rituals in early May—just when Harry Dean met his death.

It is impossible to say whether Harry Dean's death was simply an unusual accident. It is doubtful that Lethbridge would have accepted the theory that Dean's death was due to some unseen entity. But he might well have agreed that it was caused by a sudden and violent fear—a ghoul.

The chief problem concerning the enigmas discussed so far in this book is that they seem to have so little in common. What possible connection could there be between the disappearance

Above: *The Dowser Unmasked*, an illustration from a German work of 1704 in which the dowser is shown to be a devil, complete with tail and cloven hooves.

Above right: Mademoiselle Martin, the daughter of a merchant from Grenoble who became well-known for her dowsing abilities in the 1690s. Her success in once finding a bell in a flooded river is the subject of this engraving.

Above far right: Jacques Aymar, a well-known French dowser born in 1662, is shown dowsing over four prisoners to discover which of them was a thief and murderer.

72

of a British regiment into a cloud, the strange loss of electric power in the Bermuda Triangle, and a feeling of "something nasty" on a Dorset beach? Many of the writers on the Bermuda Triangle talk about "space-time paradoxes," and suggest that the disappearing planes and ships might have tumbled into another dimension. Link this with dowsing experiences and we may be getting somewhere. The whole idea of strange forces connected with fields—whether these are ancient Chinese dragon paths or Lethbridge's ghouls—seems to offer some *practical* possibility of investigation. There is nothing to prevent every reader of this book from making himself a dowsing rod or a pendulum, and checking whether these ideas have any basis in fact.

Lethbridge himself embarked upon such a careful course of experiment, and his results are startling and fascinating. I myself have performed some of the simpler experiments, and can confirm that they actually work.

In a book by Lethbridge called *The Monkey's Tail*, the reader can find a whole table of "rates" for various objects and qualities—milk, youth, apple, iron, alcohol, and so on. But he may be puzzled to see that the table includes such concepts as north, east, south, and west, life, death, danger, and time. How on earth do you hold the pendulum above "time"? Lethbridge explains that all you have to do is to think about a concept clearly, and then lengthen the string of the pendulum, which can be wound on a bobbin, until it gyrates. For example, if you think of the concept of anger, the pendulum will gyrate at 40 inches precisely, because 40 inches is the rate for anger. This idea may be less absurd than it sounds. Whenever you "see" anything, you do so by *firing* your attention toward it, as you might fire an arrow at a target. For example, if you look at your watch while thinking of something else, you simply do not register the time. We have all had the experience of staring straight at an object we have been looking for, and not seeing it. In order to see it, we need to reach out toward it with an

Above: the signboard of a contemporary dowser who practices in the western part of England.

Above: a 16th-century dowser searching for metals. In works of the period dealing with mining, there are frequent references to dowsers and their abilities. Right: a dowser looking for buried treasure. His rods are designed to be receptive to electrical currents from the ground, and they cross each other when a "find" is registered beneath that point.

"intention." Lethbridge is merely saying that this intention is the essential element in the use of the pendulum. The force that makes the pendulum circle or the dowsing rod twist in your hand may exist "out there," but it connects up with something in your mind.

Lethbridge discovered that the rate for "life" is 20 inches. The rate for death, which is twice that, appeared to be a limit, since all substances tested had rates between one and 40. There was, however, a curious paradox. Lethbridge found that if he went beyond the limit of 40 inches, the pendulum reacted again when it hit a figure that was the sum of something's own rate plus 40. For example, when testing a male the pendulum reacted at 24 inches, but it also reacted at 64 inches—40 plus 24. Similarly all the other substances reacted at their own rate, and at their own rate plus 40.

In making this discovery Lethbridge encountered an even stranger phenomenon. If you take an object such as a walnut salad bowl, place it on the floor, and hold the pendulum over it, you will get a reaction at the specified rate for walnut: $10\frac{1}{2}$ inches. If you lengthen the pendulum to $50\frac{1}{2}$ inches, you again get a reaction, *but not in the same place*. It is as if there were another salad bowl at the side of the real physical object. Lethbridge declares that this is always so—as if the object had a second position in another plane.

Equally curious is the test for "time." The pendulum fails to give a reaction for time below 40 inches. But if you lengthen the string, you locate time at 60 inches (40 plus 20, or the rate

for death plus the rate for life). Lethbridge makes the strange observation that the time thus located "appears to be static." (The pendulum gives different reactions for things that are static and things that are changing or in motion.) His conclusion is that time does not register in our physical dimension because it is always passing. But *beyond* our dimension—beyond the point of death—we encounter another kind of time that is somehow static. Lethbridge admits that he cannot begin to grasp this possibility, and that he may have reasoned incorrectly from the information supplied by the pendulum. But in that case, he has no doubt that the fault lies in him, not in the pendulum.

Admittedly, this reasoning sounds wildly absurd, and the skeptical reader will remain totally unconvinced. After all, it is only too easy to make a pendulum change its swing from an arc to a circle by some tiny unconscious movement of the fingers. Yet most people will accept the reality of dowsing, which has been seen to produce results. According to Lethbridge, the use of a pendulum enables the mind to establish contact with the "other dimension." Yet most dowsers agree that dowsing consists of tuning in to a "field." Is it possible that there are spots on the earth's surface where such fields are created by freak conditions, manifesting themselves as a kind of whirlpool in our space-time continuum? If so, we might expect objects that pass too close to be sucked into the whirlpool and to reappear later, floating on the surface of our normal time-sea. And if this idea creates a slight sense of vertigo, that is perhaps what you might expect of a whirlpool in space-time.

Above: a dowser using a map and a pendulum. Many dowsers find that their abilities are in no way impaired by working from a map, and this method of searching has obvious advantages when the site being investigated is difficult or inconvenient to reach.

Uninvited Visitors

Lough Nahooin is a small brown-colored lake in Connemara on the west coast of Ireland. At seven o'clock on the evening of February 22, 1968 Stephen Coyne, a local farmer, was walking along the shores of the lough. He was accompanied by his eight-year-old son and his dog. Stopping beside a heap of peat, Coyne saw a black object in the water, and assumed that his dog had gone for a swim. When he whistled, however, the dog came running from the opposite direction and, on seeing the black object, began to bark furiously. The farmer looked more closely and saw that the object was some kind of animal with a long neck

There are strange tales of living creatures unrecorded in any natural history book, some of them so fantastic that even the observers themselves find them nearly impossible to believe—except that they insist that they saw *something*. There are even reports that seem to describe beings not of this world at all. Do we have uninvited visitors?

Right: a 19th-century painting of the *Ride of the Valkyries*. In Norse mythology the Valkyries were attendants of the chief god Odin, and rode into battles to choose the dead heroes worthy of dining with him in the afterlife. Today there are those who suggest that legends of the Valkyries, who wear strange headgear, are a folk memory of a visit by outer-space people in space helmets.

"The monster had no eyes... but horns on the top of its head"

and shiny black skin. When it plunged its head under the surface, two humps appeared. The farmer also caught a glimpse of a flat tail. By this time the barking of the dog had attracted the attention of the "monster;" it began to swim toward the shore, its mouth open. Alarmed for the safety of his dog, the farmer hurried toward the water. At this the creature turned and made off. The eight-year-old boy ran back to the nearby farm, and brought his mother and the four other Coyne children. The family stood at the edge of the lough watching the monster until it became too dark to see. Describing it later to an investigator, F. W. Holiday, the Coynes said the monster was about 12 feet long. It had no eyes, but there were two horns like those of a snail on top of its head.

Holiday was the author of a book on the famous Loch Ness monster, which he believed to be some kind of giant slug. From the descriptions of the Coyne family, he had no doubt that this Lough Nahooin monster was another member of the same species. Since Lough Nahooin is a mere 100 yards long—compared with the 24 miles of Loch Ness—there seemed a reasonable chance of catching the Irish lake monster. Accordingly, Holiday's team brought nets, support-buoys, and 100 yards of heavy chain to Lough Nahooin. They stretched the nets across the middle of the lake, and then rowed around the lake firing a heavy rifle into the water to rouse the monster into rushing into the nets. Nothing happened—except that Holiday developed a severe toothache. After several disappointing days, they abandoned the hunt. Nevertheless, Holiday remained convinced that the monster had been in the lake all the time—and is there still.

Holiday himself has acknowledged the obvious argument against his idea. Lough Nahooin is full of trout, and if a creature even the size of a crocodile lived there, the fish would all be eaten in a matter of weeks. Perhaps, then, the Coyne family mistook an otter or a large eel for the monster. Even if that was so in this case, there have been numerous sightings of some unknown species in many of the peaty lakes in the west of Ireland. Holiday gathered further evidence from Georgina Carberry, the librarian of Clifden in Connemara. In 1954 Miss Carberry and three friends drove to nearby Lough Fadda, a mile and a half long lake, to fish for trout. They settled down on a tongue of land to have a picnic. Then they saw the monster, which at first they took to be a man swimming. The creature moved toward them in a leisurely manner, and they could see two large humps and a forked tail. They also saw a huge sharklike mouth, although none of them noticed teeth. When they became alarmed and moved away from the edge of the lake, the creature turned and swam away. Georgina Carberry found the experience so unpleasant that she kept looking back as they drove away to see if the monster was following them. She suffered from nightmares for weeks afterward, and one of her companions subsequently had a mental breakdown. Miss Carberry described the creature's movements as "wormy." Other witnesses who have reported seeing monsters in nearby lakes are generally agreed on an undulating wormlike movement.

Above: a sea serpent, depicted in a woodcut of 1560. Reports of dragonlike creatures living in water—either freshwater lakes or the open ocean—recur repeatedly, virtually on a worldwide scale.

Left: F. W. Holiday, one of the most dedicated and best known of the investigators into the possibility of unidentified creatures in Loch Ness and other similar lakes in Scotland and Ireland.

Below: one of Holiday's team at Lough Nahooin, setting nets across the lake in an attempt to capture a mysterious sluglike creature that a local family reported having seen.

THE LOCH NESS MONSTER

Left: aerial view of Loch Ness, the largest body of fresh water in Great Britain. Its mean average depth is twice that of the North Sea, and reaches 734 feet at the deepest recorded spot. Any search in the loch is greatly hampered by the peat particles brought into it by 45 mountain streams and five rivers. The lake is like a thick soup, and the deeper it goes the thicker it gets. Speculation about life in the lake—the well-known Loch Ness monster—has gone on since Saint Columba was reported to have encountered it threatening a swimmer in A.D. 565. He told it to go away, and it did.

Below left: a 1948 postcard which features Nessie, by then beloved and familiar to the public.

Below: a typical photograph showing a vague object identified as the Loch Ness monster. Although photographers and observers have spent countless hours camped by the edge of the lake, there are no unambiguous photographs. This one was taken by one of the most enthusiastic Nessie-watchers, an Englishman named Frank Searle. He has spent years camped at the lakeside, spending up to 19 hours a day looking for the monster.

Our original objection remains to all such monster sightings: how could creatures of the size described exist in these tiny lakes? Many writers on the Loch Ness monster have made the same point. It is true that Loch Ness is 24 miles long, but it is only a mile wide. There would have to be more than one monster for the species to survive, and a colony of monsters would soon eat all the fish and die of starvation.

A few months after his visit to Lough Nahooin, Holiday was browsing through a book on Babylonian history by Sir Wallis Budge. He came across a Babylonian creation myth that described how the god Anu had created marshes. According to the ancient text, "the marshes created the Worm. And the Worm said: '. . . Let me drink amongst the teeth, and set me on the gums, that I may devour the blood of the teeth . . .'" Holiday recalled the strange and persistent toothache that had begun as soon as he arrived at Lough Nahooin, and which vanished as soon as he left the area. He experienced a sudden absurd suspicion: could it be that the monster was not a creature of flesh and blood, *but some kind of a ghost*?

Of course, the idea sounds preposterous. But before we dismiss it, let us recall a point made by T. C. Lethbridge: a ghost is not necessarily a supernatural spirit. The image you see on your television screen is a kind of ghost. It is a mere "specter" of something that may be happening in a studio many miles away. Lethbridge firmly believed that the ghost of the woman he saw near his home was some kind of "tape recording." Carl G. Jung, one of the most eminent psychologists of our time, made a similar suggestion about flying saucers. He thought that the saucers could be *projections* of some deep unconscious need in mankind. Jung does not mean that UFOs are mere illusions, based on some form of wishful thinking; he means that some deep religious craving in the subconscious mind of the whole race may somehow project the image of UFOs so that they actually appear in the outside world.

Holiday reached the conclusion that UFOs and monsters share the characteristic of being less solid and real than they look. At least he can claim to have had experience of both. In his book *The Dragon and the Disk* he describes a number of sightings of UFOs and of the Loch Ness monster. The first UFO he saw, when fishing on the Welsh coast, resembled a cloud "of shiny blue-grey cotton wool," [absorbent cotton] orbiting slowly in a circle. A week later, driving along a mountain road in Wales, he saw another such "cloud" and examined it through binoculars. The cloud was oval and about 25 feet long. Similar clouds have been described by witnesses over Loch Ness.

Holiday was fascinated by how often the two themes of "dragons" and "disks" appear in ancient cultures. He points out that many Bronze Age barrows, when seen from the air, resemble flying saucers. Drawings of disklike objects are found all over the world in caves of the Paleolithic period between 12,000 and 30,000 years ago. Equally common are drawing of worms or dragons. These also turn up frequently in carvings in old churches, and usually appear to symbolize the power of evil. Holiday's suggestion is that some of our remote ancestors

worshipped disks, while others worshipped dragons or serpents. The disks usually seem to be associated with good, and the dragons are almost invariably evil.

Anyone who has ever taken an interest in UFOs knows that they have a curious habit of appearing and disappearing. Ivan Sanderson, who also wrote on the Bermuda Triangle, described a UFO he and his wife saw in 1958. It was an oval object that "was sort of flashing on and off, from almost total diaphaneity to complete solidity, at about three flashes per second." That is to say, it appeared solid one moment, and almost invisible the next. There have been dozens of reports of flying saucers that have "vanished into thin air"—giving rise to the theory that they have slipped out of our space-time into another dimension. Creatures like the Loch Ness monster seem to have the same irritating characteristic. For the past few years a Loch Ness investigation team has kept constant watch at the loch throughout the summer, with their cameras loaded. During that time the monster has been seen repeatedly— by members of the team and others—yet hardly ever photographed with any degree of success. Frustrated monster-watchers have sometimes wondered if the creature has a malicious sense of humor.

Many psychical investigators have entertained the same suspicion about ghosts and poltergeists. Holiday describes a case that he investigated in Wales. Some friends had leased a house that appeared to be haunted. Electric lights turned themselves on and off, footsteps walked down empty corridors, voices were heard, and a shadowy figure was seen in the house and the garden. The Society for Psychical Research was consulted. They suggested that the various phenomena might be due to the vibration of the tides *five miles away*. Careful experiment convinced Holiday that no amount of vibration could make a light turn itself on—as it did when he sat drinking tea with his friends. Nor could vibrations cause doorknobs to turn as they often did when no one was standing anywhere near them.

Anybody who has experienced such strange events at first hand is bound to ask himself the question: where do ghosts or poltergeists come from? Are they projections of our subconscious mind or of someone else's subconscious mind? Are they actually here, in our world, but invisible except in special

Below: one of the many recent photographs of a UFO. This one was taken in Oklahoma in 1965 by Alan Smith, who was then a newsboy. The evidence for the existence of UFOs has been almost endlessly argued pro and con. Although there are many obvious cranks among the ranks of the UFO-sighters, even the most skeptical investigators have agreed that some expert observers seem to be genuinely convinced that they saw something in the sky.

Left: a carving on the end of a church pew in Somerset, England depicts a fierce battle with a dragon—symbolic of good overcoming evil. Holiday has demonstrated that the theme of dragons and disks recurs in the mythology and artifacts of many different ancient cultures. According to Holiday and other investigators, the dragon is usually associated with wickedness in Western legends, and the disks are generally considered a symbol of goodness.

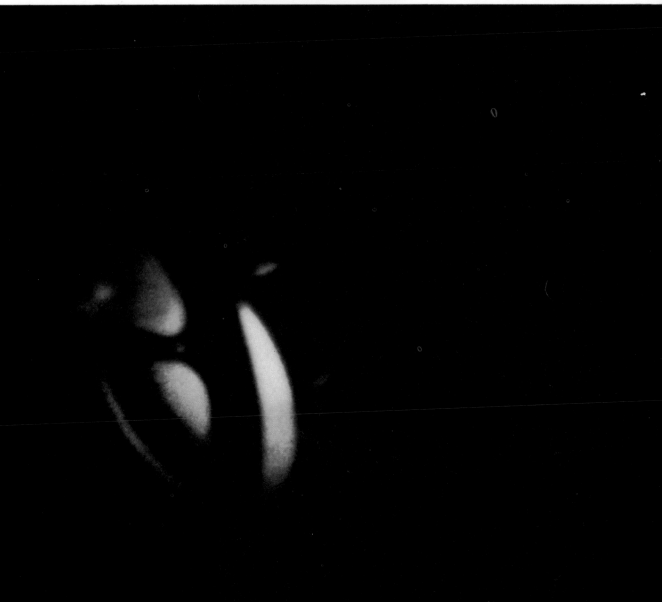

Above: a photograph of the "Warminster Thing" taken by Gordon Faulkner, a young factory worker, on August 29, 1965. At about that time there were several strange events in the area and many sightings of UFOs, some disk-shaped and some cigar-shaped.

Right: clearing up after the 1966 disaster in Aberfan, Wales, in which 144 people, almost all of them children, died. Holiday says that he saw a UFO moving off in the direction of Aberfan almost exactly two weeks before a coal slag heap slid on the town.

circumstances? Do they exist in some way outside our normal dimensions of space and time? If so, do they originate in that same world that many ufologists believe to be the home of flying saucers? In the present state of our knowledge, we cannot answer these questions; but we can go on asking them and trying to find the answers.

Holiday admits that his own case is far from complete. Some essential pieces of the jigsaw are missing. What he is suggesting—purely as a working hypothesis—is that there could be some connection between UFOs, lake monsters, and certain psychical phenomena. The dragon and disk symbolism that occurs in so many pre-Christian religions seems to indicate that the ancient priesthoods recognized the connection. We do not yet possess the knowledge to penetrate their secrets. But we do have an ever increasing mass of data about modern dragons and disks, some of which suggests a definite link between UFOs and psychical phenomena. Holiday cites the case of Annabelle Randall who, on the night of October 7, 1965, was driving her fiancé John Plowman back to his home near Warminster about 15 miles from Stonehenge. Toward midnight they approached a railroad bridge near Heytesbury, Wiltshire, where there had been a number of fatal road accidents. In the beam of their headlights they saw a body sprawled at the roadside with its legs in the road. When they stopped the car and went to investigate, the body vanished. An hour later on her return journey, Miss Randall again passed

under the bridge. As she did so, she saw a large orange ball that shot into the sky. At the same time, she saw two figures walking along the road toward her. They wore dark clothes and some sort of headgear, and the lower half of their bodies glistened as if wet.

A month later, a retired Royal Air Force Group Captain and his wife had a similar experience when driving about a mile from the bridge at 1:30 in the morning. They saw a tall figure wearing a mask. Then a man staggered out of the hedge. He was covered in blood, and seemed to be an accident victim. By the time they had stopped the car and reversed, both men had vanished. The Group Captain told his story to the Features Editor of the *Warminster Journal* and to a BBC producer, but asked for his name to be withheld.

Holiday makes an interesting suggestion concerning such "phantom accidents." He observes that more UFOs have been seen in the area around Stonehenge than anywhere else in Britain. He adds that the first UFO he sighted over the Welsh coast moved away due east, toward the little mining village of Aberfan. It was there on October 21, 1966—just 13 days after his sighting—that a massive coal tip slid downhill, killing 128 children and 16 adults. Holiday points out that in Celtic and Norse mythology, the souls of those who died in battle are conducted to the Underworld by special messengers of the dead, called *Valkyries* by the Norse. These messengers are usually represented as wearing unusual headgear—a kind of

Below: *The Procession of the Valkyries* by Gaston Bussière. There is an interesting suggestion that the old myths involving the Valkyries might have been a dim memory of UFOs and their odd inhabitants appearing before a disaster. Do they still visit?

Left: kourrigannes—dreaded fairies in Breton tradition—in a wild dance around ancient stone monuments. Many old monuments in in Europe are associated with tales of fairies—the old frighteningly unpredictable fairies, not the winsome fluttering version of nursery illustration—as well as with pagan ceremonies and mystic rites of all kinds. Can it be that some of the charged energy reported in these monuments is the bioenergy of their frenzied rituals?

pointed helmet. Is it conceivable, Holiday asks, that the strange figures seen on the Warminster road were also "messengers of the dead," whose business is to perform some kind of psychic first aid on those who have died in violent accidents? And might the old legends of Valkyries and similar creatures have been based on the visitation of UFOs and on their strange inhabitants?

Curiously enough, T. C. Lethbridge arrived independently at a similar theory shortly before his death in 1973. He published it in his last book, *The Legend of the Sons of God*. Lethbridge is careful to state that his conclusions are purely speculative, but they have a bearing on Holiday's Valkyries and it is worth examining what Lethbridge has to say on the subject.

Lethbridge's starting point is the mystery of ancient stone monuments like Stonehenge and the Merry Maidens. When he tested a stone at the Merry Maidens with his pendulum, the reaction was violent. Other prehistoric monuments produced a similar reaction. Lethbridge became convinced that the power that apparently emanates from such monoliths is a form of

Left: Druids preparing to celebrate the summer solstice at Stonehenge, which has been a center of mystic rituals since prehistoric times. Right: sacred objects, among them the four elements and a crown of oak leaves used in the ceremonies. Below: a "presider," a non-Druid selected to be honored for a significant contribution to the arts or sciences, being crowned during the High Noon ceremony at the summer solstice. He wears the Druid headdress and robes.

energy that comes from living creatures. He calls it *bio-energy*, or bio-electricity. He believes that such energy can be generated by the frenzied kind of dancing that forms part of many ancient religious rituals. This bio-energy, he maintains, can be stored in stone monoliths and in trees—and it was a vital link with visitors from other worlds.

In recent years, writers like Erich von Däniken have popularized the theory that the earth was visited by flying saucers in the remote past, and that accounts of these visits can be found in many ancient texts including the Bible. Lethbridge had already completed his *Legend of the Sons of God* when a friend sent him von Däniken's first book *Chariots of the Gods?*, containing this now-famous theory. Lethbridge's first reaction was to decide not to publish his own book. Then it struck him that many of his own conclusions differ so fundamentally from von Däniken's that it would be a pity to consign them to the wastepaper basket.

Lethbridge had concluded that monuments like Stonehenge were intended to be signal beacons for some form of spacecraft. He suggests that the inhabitants of the UFOs understood the uses to which bio-energy could be put. They therefore encouraged the men of the Bronze Age to build these giant monuments, and to keep them highly charged with bio-energy to enable the UFOs to home in on them.

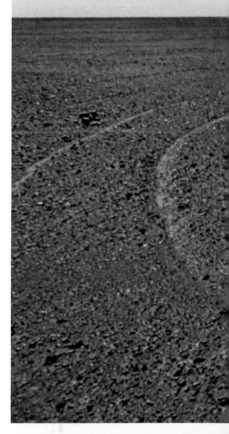

While we must admit that Lethbridge's theory sounds wildly speculative, we have to acknowledge that such monuments as Stonehenge present us with a baffling mystery. When modern engineers set about replacing one of the giant lintels at Stonehenge, they had the full benefit of modern cranes and lifting equipment, and the operation was still a difficult and costly one. Yet we know that our primitive ancestors not only succeeded in erecting these gigantic stones, but that they had transported them enormous distances across wild and rugged country. Either the ancient builders possessed a far higher degree of engineering knowledge than the traditional view of their culture suggests—or they were instructed and directed by beings from a more advanced civilization. The immense avenues of standing stones in Carnac, Brittany, present a similar problem. It is worth noting that their layout strongly supports the idea that they were aerial markers.

If the Earth had been visited by aliens in the distant past, where did these beings come from? There is a certain amount of evidence in ancient mythology—for example, in the legends of Easter Island—that suggests that the answer might be Mars or Venus or both. The astronomer Professor Carl Sagan believes that Mars could have been inhabited as recently as 1000 years ago. However, Lethbridge has another suggestion to make, based on the evidence of the pendulum. His suggestion appeared to indicate that there are other levels of existence beyond this one. If there are other levels, says Lethbridge, is it not conceivable that there are people living on them?

In addition to the evidence of the pendulum, Lethbridge produces many arguments in favor of these other levels based on out-of-the-body experiences and the power of certain mediums to foretell the future. He puts forward another

Above: the German mathematician and geographer Maria Reich stands among some of the curious markings on the vast Nazca Plain in Peru. She has spent over 40 years surveying these markings. This particular set of furrows, viewed from a plane, is the spiral tail of an Amazonian monkey.

Left: Maria Reich taking her meticulous measurements. The plain is covered with a thin layer of sand and pebbles that are oxidized into a warm brown color and have a very fragile texture. Underneath lies a bed of white alluvium, and a step on the brown surface will leave a white footprint for the ages. The patterns on the plain were formed by drawing lines on the brown surface, some narrow as a mountain path and others as broad as a modern airport runway.

Right: an aerial view of part of the plain, which extends over 100,000 acres. Because the figures can only be properly seen from the air, it has been suggested they are landing signals for ancient UFOs.

fascinating idea. The pendulum appears to show that the other levels possess a higher rate of vibration than our earthly level, as if their energies were of a higher frequency. Yet the pendulum apparently enables us to establish some sort of contact with these levels. Perhaps, Lethbridge suggests, it might be possible for scientists to construct a machine that would alter our vibrational rate, and so make these levels directly accessible. Such a machine, he says, "would necessitate some kind of dynamo to produce a field of force around the experimenters. . . ."

Lethbridge would therefore seem to agree with F. W. Holiday and many ufologists that Unidentified Flying Objects could originate on some other plane of existence. Lethbridge also points out that if these other levels are characterized by a higher vibrational rate of energy, then creatures from these levels could actually be walking among us now—completely invisible to us. They would become visible only if their vibrational rate were suddenly slowed down. This can be grasped by means of a simple analogy. If a train on which you are riding goes through a station too fast, you cannot read the name of the station. If the train was traveling extremely fast, you would not even notice the station. On the other hand, to beings on these other planes, we would appear to be traveling much more slowly than they—as if we were living in slow motion—and we would therefore be clearly visible to them. *They* could visit us by slowing down their vibrational rate, but we cannot at present visit them—except possibly by dying.

It is interesting to note that, if Lethbridge is right, our thought vibrations would have difficulty in grasping the nature of reality because they are too slow. But the faculty we call intuition seems to operate instantaneously, on a higher wavelength. This may explain why intuition has the power to grasp complex realities beyond the range of our everyday thought.

Lethbridge's machine for traveling to other planes sounds like pure science fiction. Yet there are many students of ufology who are convinced that such a machine has actually been built and tested. Unfortunately, one of the most important witnesses, the astronomer and mathematician Morris K. Jessup, is dead. Jessup taught at the University of Michigan, and was sent by the Carnegie Institute to study the Inca remains in Peru and the Aztec ruins in Mexico. The study of these ancient constructions led him to the conclusion that they might well have been erected with the aid of outer space visitors, whose aim was partly to create landing markers for spacecraft. He published his theory in 1955 in *The Case for the UFO*, one of the first great classics on the subject of flying saucers. In this book, Jessup also suggested that many of the strange disappearances of ships and planes in the Bermuda Triangle—and mysteries such as those of the *Mary Celeste* and *Ellen Austin*—could have been due to some kind of UFO activity.

After the publication of his book, Jessup was contacted by someone who claimed to be a survivor of an incredible experiment conducted by the U.S. Navy in 1943. Known as "the Philadelphia Experiment," it was supposed to have resulted in the death of some participants and the mental breakdown of others. When Jessup began to investigate the affair, the Navy asked him if he would be interested in working on a similar project. Jessup declined. In 1959 Jessup was found dead in his car, asphyxiated by exhaust gas. There are some who believe that his suicide was staged, and that he was killed before he could publicize ideas arising out of the experiment.

In *The Mysterious Unknown*, Robert Charroux cites another version of the Philadelphia Experiment, as reported from the Soviet Union. The Soviets apparently believed that the U.S. Navy was investigating some magnetic version of the Moebius Strip. This Strip is a "one-sided" ring of paper, and is easy to make. You simply take a long strip of paper, give one of its ends a half-twist, and then glue the two ends of the strip together to form a ring. If you wish to verify that this strip has only one side, take a pencil, and draw a line down the center of the strip. You will find that, without having to turn the ring inside out, you can continue the line until it has rejoined its beginning. If you take a pair of scissors and cut along the penciled line, the strip will unfold into one large ring instead of the two interlinked rings that most people expect.

According to the Soviet version, the vessel used in the Philadelphia Experiment was a submarine, and the "Moebius strip" consisted of a powerful magnetic field. As the submarine pursued its course around this invisible strip—turning over completely in the course of each revolution—some electronic device was used to cut the field in two, as if with a pair of scissors. At this point the submarine vanished, to reappear miles away. In the Soviet version, as in the American one, some of the crew died and others became insane. The story was told by Professor Doru Todericiu, who claimed to have read it in official reports published in the Soviet Union.

Whatever the real story behind the Philadelphia Experiment, it is interesting that both the Soviet and American versions are based on the use of a magnetic field of unusual power. There is also a postscript to Jessup's account of the experiment, as related by Dr. Manson Valentine, that has the touch of authenticity. Jessup was apparently told that, on two occasions, the ship's binnacle (compass box) burst into flames as it was being carried ashore, with disastrous results to the carrier.

We know that magnetism affects compasses—but why should it cause a wooden box to burst into flame? The answer may well lie in Lethbridge's ideas about bio-electricity. Lethbridge had said from the first that bio-electricity can be generated by dancing. Perhaps this is related to spontaneous combustion. For example a girl, dancing in a London nightclub with her boyfriend, suddenly erupted into flames, and died on her way to the hospital. There were no flames in the room. Her dancing partner declared that the flames seemed to burst from the girl's back, chest, and shoulders, setting her hair on fire. Hundreds of similar cases have been recorded. Like all other energies known to man, bio-electricity seems to have its dangerous side. But it may also provide science with another angle in the investigation of the strange unknown powers of the human psyche.

The Philadelphia Experiment

Can a ship be made invisible? If rumors circulating since 1943 are to be believed, the U.S. Navy tried an experiment to do just that—and succeeded at the cost of the lives or sanity of the crew.

The story goes that it happened in Philadelphia. A hazy green light began to creep into a Navy ship moored there. When the vessel was filled with the green haze, it disappeared entirely. At the same moment the ship was seen in the harbor of Norfolk, nearly 1000 miles away. The vessel continued to vanish and reappear at sea for a time, crew members vanishing and reappearing with it.

How was the disappearance of the ship brought about? This is hard to answer because all documents in the case have been kept top secret. But it is believed by many that the experimenters created an incredibly strong magnetic field in and around the vessel with special generators.

A report of the test came to the young scientist Dr. Morris K. Jessup, who had been studying the idea of inducing invisibility. According to this report, 16 crew members died and six went insane as a result of the program. Dr. Jessup himself committed suicide before his investigation of The Philadelphia Experiment was done.

6

Jinxes and Curses

The year was 1928. The city, Kobe, Japan. A middle-aged English couple, the C. J. Lamberts, stood in front of a junk shop window. "That's what I'd like," said Marie Lambert, pointing to a tiny statuette of a half-naked fat man seated on a cushion. She recognized the laughing man as Ho-tei, the Japanese god of Good Luck. "Let's find out what he costs," said her husband, as they walked into the shop. They were pleasantly surprised to find that the statuette was cheap, even though it was made of ivory. It seemed almost too good to be true. Back on their cruise ship, the Lamberts examined their purchase closely. The sta-

Right: Ho-tei, the Japanese god of good luck. However, one tiny statuette of Ho-tei in 1928 brought nothing but bother to an English couple that bought it. From a purely rational standpoint it is obviously impossible for objects to exert any direct influence for good or evil over human beings. A carved piece of ivory is only a piece of ivory; an automobile is just a mass of machinery. But we have all heard of the malignant influence some objects have apparently cast over their possessors—and how many of us, having discovered that each of four previous owners of a house came to a sudden and unexpected death, would willingly be the fifth to take possession?

"Their tooth-aches...always occurred when Ho-tei was in their cabin"

tuette had the creamy color of old ivory, and was beautifully carved. As far as they could see, its only minor imperfection was a small hole underneath. The carver had apparently used the base of an elephant's tusk for the statue, and there was a tiny hole where the nerve of the animal's tooth had ended. This had been plugged neatly with an ivory peg. Altogether, the statuette seemed to be one of those rare bargains that tourists dream about.

Marie Lambert stowed the statuette in her luggage, and the ship sailed to Manila. On the second day out, Mrs. Lambert began to suffer from a toothache. The ship's doctor prescribed pain killers, but they did little good. The next 12 days were miserable for both the Lamberts. In Manila, before Mrs. Lambert could visit a dentist, she and her husband contracted an unpleasant fever whose chief symptom was pain in all the joints. When Marie Lambert finally got to a dentist, his drill slipped and drove through to the nerve of her tooth, increasing her pain instead of curing it.

On the next lap of the voyage, which took the ship to Australia, the god of luck was somehow transferred to Mr. Lambert's luggage. The following day, he was prostrated with an agonizing toothache. In Cairns, Australia he went to a dentist, who told him there was nothing wrong with his teeth. In fact, the ache had stopped while he was at the dentist's. But it started again as soon as he got back to his cabin. Two days later, he consulted another dentist, and the same thing happened. In Brisbane, he ordered a dentist to start pulling out his teeth, and to keep on pulling until the pain stopped. When the first tooth came out, the pain went away. It started again as soon as Lambert returned to the ship.

In Sydney the Lamberts left their luggage in bond. The toothache ceased. On the voyage to New Zealand, the luggage was in their cabin only once, when they repacked; Lambert's toothache started again. Then the luggage went to the hold, and the pain stopped. In New Zealand while on shore, he had no toothache. There was only one short bout of toothache on the continuing trip to Chile—when the Lamberts repacked their luggage in the cabin. In the United States, the couple visited Lambert's mother. She was so delighted with Ho-tei that they made her a present of the little god. When her excellent teeth started aching a few hours later, she handed back the gift saying that she felt it was "bad medicine." The Lamberts still did not connect Ho-tei with their toothaches.

Their first suspicion occurred on the way across the Atlantic to Britain. A fellow passenger who was interested in ivory borrowed Ho-tei overnight to show her husband. In the morning, she told the Lamberts that she and her husband had both had toothaches. The Lamberts thought about their toothaches, and realized that they had always occurred when Ho-tei was in their cabin. Marie Lambert wanted to throw the statuette overboard. Her husband was afraid that the god might retaliate by rotting every tooth in their heads. So they took Ho-tei back to London with them. Lambert took the figure to an oriental art shop and showed it to the Japanese manager, who immediately offered to buy it. Lambert explained

96

that he could not take money for the statuette, and he described the troubles it seemed to have caused. The manager sent for an old man in Japanese national costume, and the two men examined the figure carefully. From what they told him, Lambert gathered that Ho-tei was a temple god. In the East, the statues of such gods are sometimes given "souls"—small medallions hidden inside them. This probably explained the ivory plug in the base of the figure. The old Japanese man placed Ho-tei in a shrine at the end of the shop and lit joss sticks in front of it. Then, with an expression of awe, he bowed Lambert out of the shop.

In the end, C. J. Lambert derived some small profit from his uncomfortable adventure. He recounted it in a travel book that made good sales. But he never revisited the London art shop.

Lambert's understandable assumption was that the god of luck had been taking revenge on unbelievers who had removed him from his temple. Yet there could be another explanation for this strange affair.

Around the Iron Age fort in Sidbury Castle in southern England, T. C. Lethbridge picked up many rounded flint pebbles of the kind commonly found on beaches. It seemed unlikely that the sea had transported the stones to the fort, which stands on the top of a hill three miles inland. However, the stones were like those used as slingshot in Iron Age times. Lethbridge tested the stones with a pendulum whose string extended to 24 inches—the male length. There was a strong reaction. He tested them again at 40 inches—the rate for anger, war, and death. Once more the reaction was strong.

Lethbridge possessed some similar sling stones from the Iron Age camp in Wandlebury, south of Cambridge. These also gave the reaction for maleness, but not for war or anger. Stones of the same type collected from the beach gave no reaction either for maleness or war.

Lethbridge's conclusion was that the Wandlebury stones had only been used for practice shots—which seems likely, since Wandlebury had been an army camp in the Iron Age. The Sidbury stones had been used in actual warfare. Both groups of stones retained the impression of maleness caused by the men who had handled them. As a further test, Lethbridge took some of the stones from the beach and threw them against a wall. They then responded to the male rate of 24 inches. Stones thrown by his wife only responded to the female rate—29 inches. Some kind of thought energy—or biological electricity—had apparently impressed itself on the stones like a seal. And it seemed to last indefinitely.

According to Lethbridge, the pendulum can also reveal the *date* at which the thought field was implanted in an object. This is done by counting the number of times the pendulum revolves over the object before returning to its normal oscillation. Lethbridge established a date of 320 B.C. for all the Sidbury stones, and 220 B.C. for those from Wandlebury.

Lethbridge used a pendulum to establish who had last handled the stones. But there are certain human beings who can achieve the same result simply by contact with an object. They

The Doll with Growing Hair

Does a place of worship have more intense thought fields than ordinary buildings? Can this explain the incredible case of the doll with human hair that keeps on growing?

The story comes from northern Japan and started in 1938. In that year Eikichi Suzuki took a ceramic doll to the temple in the village of Monji-Saiwai Cho for safekeeping. It had been a treasured possession of his beloved sister Kiku, who had died 19 years before at the age of three. Suzuki kept it carefully in a box with the ashes of his dead sister.

Suzuki went off to World War II and didn't return for the doll until 1947. When he opened the box in the presence of the priest, they discovered that the doll's hair had grown down to its shoulders. A skin specialist from the Hokkaido University medical faculty said it was human hair.

The doll was placed on the altar, and its hair continued to grow. It is still growing, and is now almost waist length. The temple has become a place of pilgrimage for worshippers who believe the doll is a spiritual link with Buddha.

The priest of Monji-Saiwai Cho thinks that the little girl's soul somehow continues to live through the doll she loved so much.

are called *psychometrists*. Two of the best-known modern psychometrists, Peter Hurkos and Gerard Croiset, have achieved considerable publicity by aiding the police in the investigation of crimes. By holding some object associated with the crime, such as a murder weapon, they have been able to describe the crime, and often the criminal.

In the 1840s the Frenchman Alexis Didier revealed similar powers. A report in the British *Medical Times* of July 8, 1844 tells how Didier was given a small leather case belonging to a certain Colonel Llewellyn. Didier placed the case against his stomach, and was then able to tell the owner that it contained a piece of bone—the colonel's own bone. He went on to describe in detail the incident in which the colonel had been wounded, even specifying the number of wounds he had received. The records of the Society for Psychical Research contain dozens of similar cases. These suggest that psychometry is a fairly common human faculty—as common perhaps as the ability to dowse, although less developed in most human beings.

What would have happened if Alexis Didier had held the statue of Ho-tei? He might have experienced some of the fear and agony of a dying elephant—and perhaps the appalling pain of having a tusk removed before death came. For a man of Didier's sensitivity, the horror might have been almost unbearable. In less sensitive human beings, the tooth-fragment might have induced a milder form of psychic disturbance that manifested itself as severe toothache. If so, according to Lethbridge's theory, the statue of Ho-tei would still be capable of causing toothache in another thousand years.

It is worth recalling that F. W. Holiday complained of a severe toothache during his expedition to Lough Nahooin in search of monsters, and that he subsequently discovered a Babylonian text describing a supernatural worm whose activities include "devouring the blood of the teeth." Is it conceivable that certain negative psychic forces manifest themselves in the form of toothache.

If the question sounds absurd, it is largely because we have ceased to think in terms of negative psychic forces. The peoples of primitive tribes say that a person who experiences continual misfortune is "accursed." We would call him "accident prone." Our classification implies that proneness to accidents arises from a person's own carelessness or nervous tension. We have all known people who seem to attract bad luck—the kind of people who happen to be walking past when the window cleaner drops his bucket. These people appear to be suffering from other people's carelessness, or from plain undeserved misfortune. Yet we still have the feeling that there is some connection between this kind of ill-luck and the personality of the sufferer. There may be something about the attitude of such people—a certain expectation that the worst will happen. This raises the interesting question of whether the accident is somehow triggered by their subconscious attitude. Everything we learn about the power of the mind suggests that thought fields may be altogether more influential than we have hitherto recognized.

Above: Sidbury Hill, site of an Iron Age fort in Wiltshire, England. Lethbridge used a dowsing pendulum in this area to identify rounded flint pebbles as having been used as slingshot thousands of years ago. The pebbles responded to the pendulum when at a length of 24 inches, which is the male rate, and also at the special rate for war.

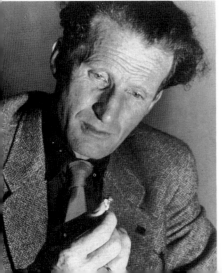

Left: Gerard Croiset, a Dutch psychometrist who by holding an object is apparently able to receive a flood of impressions about the object, its history, and its former owners. Psychometry of this kind suggests that there may be some truth in the idea that inanimate objects can convey strong physical and atmospheric impressions.

Left: the *Scharnhorst*, shown at its launching in Germany in 1936. The ship seemed to be unlucky from the start. When only half built, the *Scharnhorst* killed 60 workmen when it rolled onto its side. Even the launching was unpromising: the ship had slipped into the water the night before the formal ceremony at which Hitler himself was in attendance.

Above: the *Scharnhorst* dashing up the British Channel with the *Gneisenau* and the *Prinz Eugen* in February, 1942, when the three ships managed to elude the British.

Left: the British bombing the *Scharnhorst* in Brest in 1942. Both the *Scharnhorst* and the *Gneisenau* were damaged then. This forced the German decision to move the battleships to safety by the daring dash up the Channel.

The psychic investigator and journalist Edward Russell has suggested that there may be a connection between negative thought fields and the "curses" that appear to surround certain objects like the statuette of Ho-tei. Like Lethbridge, he believes that thought fields can implant themselves in objects, rather as magnetism or static electricity does, and create the same kind of patterns that an electric field can produce on a magnetic recording tape. Lethbridge had advanced the theory that negative thought fields—or ghouls as he called them—can imprint themselves on the magnetic field of water, and there is some evidence that ghouls may also imprint themselves on objects. We have already seen that the *Mary Celeste* was dogged by bad luck from the moment of her launching, and

Below: *The Sinking of the Scharnhorst*, a painting by C. E. Turner. The ship was destroyed on the day after Christmas in 1943, with only 36 survivors out of a crew of 1900.

Bottom: the survivors being landed in England in 1944, blindfolded so that they would not be able to see dockyard installations.

few sailors doubt that there are such things as "jinxed ships." In his book on sea mysteries, *Invisible Horizons*, Vincent Gaddis writes, "There are happy, gay ships, and there are others so impregnated with evil that they must be destroyed by fire."

The particular evil ship that Gaddis had in mind was the German battleship *Scharnhorst*, launched in October 1936. When only half completed, the ship rolled onto its side, killing 60 workmen. Hitler and Goering arrived for the final launching only to discover that the ship had somehow launched itself the previous night, destroying several barges. In the *Scharnhorst*'s first major engagement—the attack on Danzig in 1939—one of the guns exploded, killing nine men, and the air supply system broke down, suffocating 12 gunners. A year later during the bombardment of Oslo, the *Scharnhorst* was badly damaged and had to be towed away. In the dark, she collided with the ocean liner *Bremen*, which settled into the river mud

and was bombed to pieces by the British. The *Scharnhorst* was repaired and set sail for the Arctic in 1943, but during the voyage she passed a British patrol vessel which her crew failed to notice. The vessel radioed a warning. Several British cruisers quickly located the *Scharnhorst* and bombarded her. The *Scharnhorst* fled, and it seemed she would escape her pursuers. But one British commander decided to try a last long shot on the off-chance of scoring a hit. The gamble paid. The *Scharnhorst* began to blaze, providing a target for more shells. The ship sank to the bottom with most of her crew. Yet the curse apparently lingered on. Weeks later, two survivors from the *Scharnhorst* were found on a beach. They were dead—killed by an emergency oil heater that had exploded when they tried to light it for warmth.

Misfortune also pursued the Lockheed Constellation airliner AHEM-4, starting on the day in July 1945 when a mechanic walked into one of the plane's propellors and was killed. Precisely one year later, on July 9, 1946, Captain Arthur Lewis died at the controls while the plane was flying in mid-Atlantic. Exactly one year after that, on July 9, 1947, a newly installed engine burst into flame shortly after take-off. The captain, Robert Norman, extinguished the flames with a mechanical fire extinguisher, but then found that the plane lacked the power to climb above the roof of an apartment building. Norman switched on the takeoff power and managed to climb out of danger. But when he tried to ease the power off again, the controls remained jammed. He and his copilot finally wrestled the controls back by sheer force, and landed the plane successfully.

July 1948 passed uneventfully. But on July 10, 1949 the airliner crashed near Chicago, killing everyone on board including Captain Robert Norman.

There are many records of houses, and even cars, that seem to bring disaster to their owners. A famous example is the car in which the Archduke Francis Ferdinand, heir to the thrones of Austria and Hungary, was assassinated in 1914—a murder that precipitated the outbreak of World War I. The Archduke's wife died with him. Shortly after the start of war, General Potiorek of the Austrian army came into possession of the car. A few weeks later he suffered a catastrophic defeat at Valjevo, and was sent back to Vienna in disgrace. He could not stand this, and he died insane.

The next owner of the car was an Austrian captain who had been on Potiorek's staff. Only nine days after taking over the car, he struck and killed two peasants, and then swerved into a tree and broke his neck.

At the end of the war, the Governor of Yugoslavia became the owner of the car. After four road accidents in four months—one of which caused him to lose an arm—he sold the car to a doctor. Six months later, the car was found upside down in a ditch. The doctor had been crushed to death inside it. The car was next sold to a wealthy jeweler who owned it for only a year before he committed suicide. After a brief spell in the hands of another doctor—who seems to have been all too anxious to get rid of it—the car was sold to a Swiss racing driver. He was killed in a race in the Italian Alps when the car threw him over a wall. The next owner was a Serbian farmer. He stalled the car one morning, and persuaded a passing carter to give him a tow. Forgetting to turn off the ignition, the farmer became the car's ninth victim when it started up, smashed the horse and cart, and overturned on a bend. A garage owner, Tibor Hirshfeld, was the car's final owner. One day, returning from a wedding with six friends, Hirshfeld tried to overtake another car at high speed. He and four of his companions were killed. The car then was taken to a Vienna museum where it has been ever since.

An example of a house that seems to bring bad luck to its tenants is the castle of Miramar near Trieste. It was built in the mid-19th century by Emperor Franz Josef of Austria, but its first occupant was his brother the Archduke Maximilian. Maximilian died in front of a firing squad in Mexico, and his wife became insane. Empress Elizabeth was the next resident of Miramar, living there with her son Rudolph. In 1889 Rudolph

Above: in the back seat of a car that seemed to be a jinx are the Austro-Hungarian Archduke Franz Ferdinand and his wife. They were assassinated in this car while riding through Sarajevo in 1914. General Potiorek, who was later affected by the car's bad luck, is in front of the duchess.

Left: the assassination. Within six weeks of the double murder half the civilized world was at war—the terrible bloodletting known as World War I had begun.

Right: the Archduke's bloodstained tunic. The left front and sleeve were slashed open by doctors who tried vainly to save his life.

Above: General Potiorek, who was in the car that day in Sarajevo, escaped harm then. But as the next owner of the car, he too was crushed by its malignant spell: within a few weeks he suffered ignominious defeat in battle, and was sent home in disgrace.

Left: the beautiful castle in Miramar, near Trieste, which brought disaster to those who were closely associated with it.

Right: the execution of the Emperor Maximilian of Mexico, the first man to occupy Castle Miramar before he renounced his Austrian imperial rights and accepted the imperial throne in Mexico. His wife, who ruled with him, lost her sanity in a frantic struggle to rally help for him in Europe when his position became desperate in Mexico.

and his mistress committed suicide, and in 1898 the Empress was assassinated by an Italian anarchist who believed in Italian liberation from Austria.

The next in line for the Austrian throne was Rudolph's cousin the Archduke Francis Ferdinand, who went to live in the beautiful castle. The Archduke and his wife were both assassinated in 1914—the murder that contributed to bringing about World War I. At the end of the war the Duke of Aosta moved into Miramar. He died in a prison camp in British East Africa during World War II. After this war two British Major Generals became residents of the castle of Miramar. Both died of heart attacks.

It has not gone unnoticed that many jinxes appear to begin with a death or deaths: workers died building the *Scharnhorst*; a mechanic was killed by a propellor of the Lockheed Constellation airliner; the Archduke Franz Ferdinand and his wife were assassinated in their car. Many sailors are convinced that the spirits of the dead are involved in jinxes. To support their contention, they point to the two most notorious jinx ships of the 19th century: the British vessels *Hinemoa* and *Great Eastern*.

On her maiden voyage in 1892, the *Hinemoa* carried a ballast of rubble from a London Graveyard. During the voyage four sailors died of typhoid. The ship's first captain went insane, the second ended in prison, the third died of alcoholism, the fourth died in mysterious circumstances in his cabin, and the fifth committed suicide—all, according to the

Left: the death of Prince Rudolf and his mistress at the hunting lodge in Mayerling in 1899. He had lived at the Castle Miramar. In apparent despair over the hopelessness of his passion for the young and beautiful Baroness Marie Vetsera, he killed her and afterward committed suicide.

Right: the assassination of the Empress Elizabeth of Austria, nine years after the death of Prince Rudolf, her only son. She was stabbed to death by an Italian nationalist and anarchist.

crew, because of the bad luck brought by the bones of the four dead crew members.

The *Great Eastern*, built by the famous Victorian engineer Isambard Kingdom Brunel, was in her time the largest—and the unluckiest—ship in the world. Brunel collapsed with a heart attack on her deck, and died soon after. A riveter and his boy assistant vanished without trace during the ship's construction. The ship proved so heavy that she defied all attempts to launch her; it took three months and dozens of hydraulic jacks to move her from her berth. On her maiden voyage, a steam escape valve was left closed, resulting in an explosion that scalded five men to death. A full account of her subsequent misfortunes—explosions, collisions, and accidents at sea—would occupy many pages. Finally, a mere 15 years after launching, she was brought back to Milford Haven in Wales, where she rusted and blocked the shipping lane. Breaking her up proved almost as difficult as building her. It was necessary to invent the wrecker's iron ball, suspended on a giant chain, to reduce her to scrap in 1889. Inside the double hull, the demolition experts discovered the skeletons of the riveter and his boy apprentice, who had vanished when the ship was being built. Few people doubted that they had discovered the cause of the ship's misfortunes.

The theory of thought fields provides a plausible alternative to the supernatural explanation. The sailors on board the *Hinemoa* knew that the ballast had been taken from a graveyard; the men who sailed the *Great Eastern* on her maiden voyage knew that a riveter and his assistant had vanished, and had possibly been sealed up in the hull. The crew of the airliner AHEM-4 knew that a mechanic had walked into the propeller and had been cut to pieces. The subsequent owners of Francis Ferdinand's car knew that the Archduke and his wife had met violent deaths in it. Therefore, assuming that in each vehicle the original tragic event itself created a negative thought field, or ghoul, does it not seem likely that their knowledge of the tragedy *predisposed* people to tune in to that field? In other words, the jinx may have been partly due to the negative thought field, and partly to the fear and nervous tension of the people involved.

Skeptics will object that fear and tension alone might have been to blame, and that the jinxes could have been entirely psychological in origin. This possibility cannot be completely ruled out. But it still leaves us with a residue of cases in which the victim knew nothing about the ghoul. C. J. and Marie Lambert had no reason to connect the statue of Ho-tei with their toothache, for example. Lethbridge put forward the theory of ghouls after he and his wife had independently experienced acute feelings of depression on an apparently peaceful beach. Lethbridge was even convinced that the field of a ghoul is sharply defined. He describes a ruined house where it was possible to step in and out of the affected area, as if there were a line drawn on the ground. The likeliest explanation would therefore seem to be that there is some sort of interaction between the negative thought field and the people who react to it.

Above: I. K. Brunel, the eminent Victorian engineer and designer of the luckless *Great Eastern*. When designed in 1853, the ship was six times the size of any vessel that had been built before.

Right: during one of the terrible storms that seemed to stalk the *Great Eastern* in its trips across the Atlantic—few of which were ever profitable—the furniture in the elegant lounge careered from one side of the room to the other. In this engraving, a cow that provided fresh milk for the passengers—at a time of no refrigeration—has broken loose and crashed through the ceiling.

Above: the *Great Eastern* afloat. It took a long and grueling series of launching attempts that lasted from early November 1857, to January 31, 1858 before the great ship finally slid into the water. Left: during a raging storm in 1861 the rudder was destroyed, and the ship wallowed in the waves, rolling at an angle of 45 degrees.

7

Secrets of the Ancients

At the Kofuku temple in Nara, Japan, a resentful priest named Kurodo decided to play an embarrassing trick on his fellow priests. At the side of a pond near the temple, Kurodo set up a placard that read: "On March 3, a dragon shall ascend from this pond." The effect was just what he had expected. News of the placard spread far and wide, and people talked of nothing but dragons. On March 3 the pond was surrounded by thousands of people from all the neighboring provinces. The day was sunny and peaceful. By noon nothing had happened, and the priests were beginning to feel worried. If no dragon appeared, they

Silent enigmatic monuments and glancing references in fragmentary remnants of ancient writings often give the disquieting sense that the numberless generations before us grasped more profound ideas than our orthodox history allows for. Were there secrets that we have lost, and are we now on the threshold of recovering them? Right: this chart and statue show the points of the body used in treatment by acupuncture. This ancient Chinese use of needles to cure pain and disease is finding a place in medical practice today.

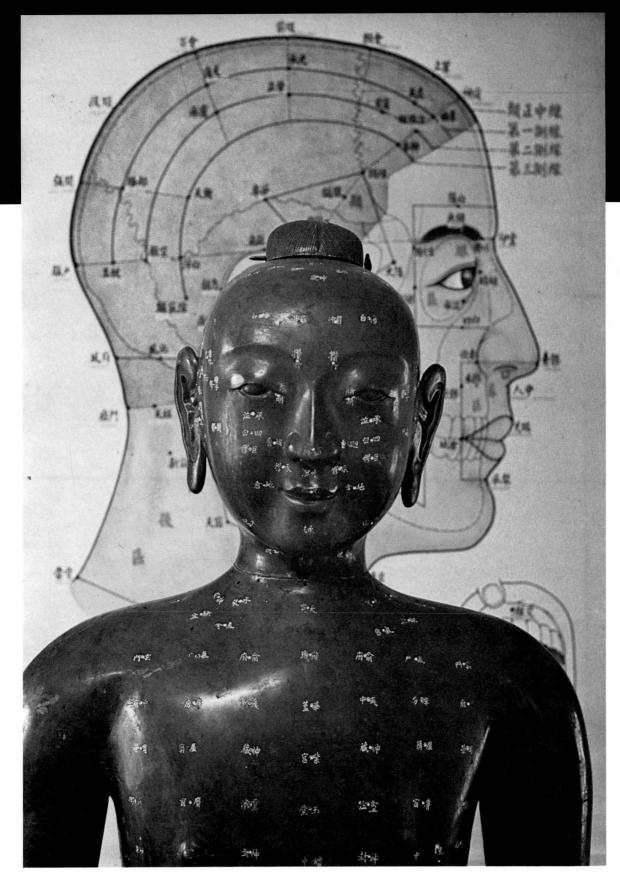

"An enormous black dragon rose out of the pond and up into the clouds"

would lose face. Suddenly, a cloud drifted across the sky. A wind sprang up. The day became darker, and a storm broke. Rain fell in torrents and lightning flashed. Before Kurodo's startled eyes, a smoky shape like an enormous black dragon rose out of the pond and up into the clouds. This story may or may not be true. It was written by the great Japanese author Akutagawa, who probably based it on a tradition of the Kofuku temple.

If Akutagawa's tale sounds incredible, consider this story, which is based on fact. In May 1727 François de Pâris, a young deacon of Paris, died of malnutrition and exhaustion. He was famous for his ascetic practices and for his charities to the poor, and his coffin was followed by hundreds of mourners. After it had been placed behind the altar of the church of St. Medard, a line of mourners filed past. One small boy, accompanied by his father, limped awkwardly on a crippled leg. As he placed a bunch of flowers on the coffin, he suddenly fell to the ground, gasping and kicking. He was apparently suffering from a fit. A few minutes later, the fit passed off. The boy sat up, and was helped to his feet. A look of astonishment came over his face. Suddenly he began to dance and shout for joy. The crippled leg—twisted since birth—was straight. As the spectators stared in amazement, an old woman shouted: "I can use it!" She was waving her cured arm, which had been paralyzed for 25 years. Many fell on their knees around the coffin of the saintly deacon and prayed.

The miracles continued, and became more astounding. All kinds of sick people touched the coffin, went into convulsions, and were cured. After the body of the saintly priest had been buried behind the high altar, the miracles took place in the cemetery outside. They were so remarkable that it is tempting to dismiss contemporary accounts of them as pure exaggerations. Yet documentary evidence—some of it written by physicians—seems to show otherwise. A Mademoiselle Coirin had cancer that had eaten away most of her breast, and the odor was so appalling that no one could go near her. After kneeling at the "saint's" tomb, she was not only cured, but also the breast showed no sign of ever having had a cancer. This sounds absurd, but doctors examined it and testified that it was so.

Cripples walked; the blind were made to see; tumors vanished. Even odder manifestations began to occur. A young girl named Gabrielle Moler went into convulsions, after which she begged the spectators to beat her with sticks. She felt no pain and showed no bruises. She had seemingly acquired some of the curious powers possessed by Hindu fakirs. Strong men could pound her with hammers, and she remained unhurt. She would thrust her face into a blazing fire, and withdraw it unburned; she would leave her feet in the fire until the shoes and socks were burned away, and withdraw her feet unscathed. Another *convulsionaire*, the name given to those who experienced convulsions at the tomb, cured horrible sores and ulcers by sucking them. One man, who had been crippled, experienced the urge to spin on one leg at tremendous speed while reading from a holy book. He did this twice a day.

Above: the pond near Kofuku temple in Japan. This setting was used for a tale about a miraculous appearance of a dragon by the great Japanese writer Akutagawa.

Right: an 18th-century engraving of Chinese sorcerers, seen with a Western eye. Note that the one in the center has an acupuncture needle inserted in his left ear.

Below: a Chinese dragon, made of ceramic tiles. In China the dragon was considered one of the four benevolent spiritual animals.

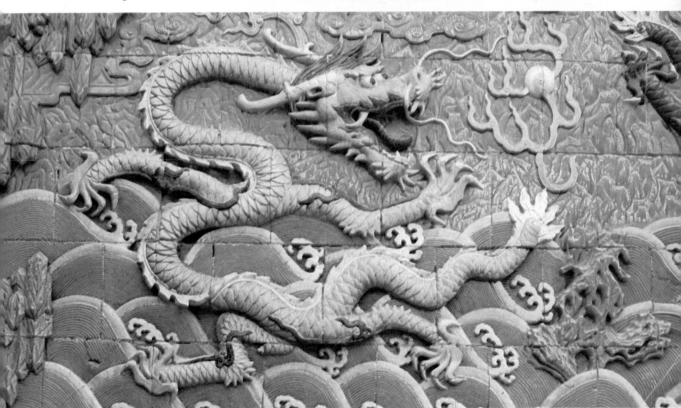

Above: a contemporary engraving showing the variety of ways in which the convulsionaires were taken in their wild hysteria.

Right: an exhibition given by the young Gabrielle Moler after she visited the tomb and fell into a convulsion. She could apparently be beaten or pricked with swords and suffer no pain, and show no marks or bruises afterward.

Above: a reliquary of about 1730 with the portrait of François de Pâris, whose grave had become the center for miracle cures. Believers in his powers behaved in such a wild way—including going into convulsions—that they were called "convulsionaires." The cemetery of St. Medard, in which de Pâris was buried, was closed by the authorities in 1732 because of the frenzied scenes.

Another convulsionaire could bounce six feet into the air, like a rubber ball, even when weighed down with heavy chains. Dozens of other visitors to the tomb rolled in convulsions or allowed spectators to beat them, without visible ill-effects.

A magistrate went to the churchyard convinced that the whole affair was a fraud. What he saw made him change his mind. He wrote books about it, and suffered imprisonment for his convictions.

The authorities were worried and embarrassed by the wild scenes at St. Medard. Françoise de Pâris, the young deacon who had started it all, had belonged to a religious sect known as the Jansenists. They denied free will and believed that people could only be saved by Divine Grace. The Jesuits, the most powerful religious order in Paris, detested the Jansenists. Through their influence, the churchyard of St. Medard was closed down in 1732, five years after the miracles began. Convulsionaires were persecuted, and the miracles ceased. Jansenism was made illegal, and finally died out.

What happened at St. Medard is similar to what happened at the Kofuku temple pond. A large number of people became deeply convinced that miracles were about to occur, and it

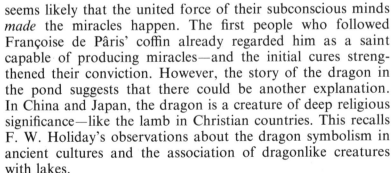

seems likely that the united force of their subconscious minds *made* the miracles happen. The first people who followed Françoise de Pâris' coffin already regarded him as a saint capable of producing miracles—and the initial cures strengthened their conviction. However, the story of the dragon in the pond suggests that there could be another explanation. In China and Japan, the dragon is a creature of deep religious significance—like the lamb in Christian countries. This recalls F. W. Holiday's observations about the dragon symbolism in ancient cultures and the association of dragonlike creatures with lakes.

It is also possible that the church of St. Medard was built on a site that, like Stonehenge and other megaliths, is a point at which dragon paths or ley lines meet. This would explain the concentration of magnetic powers there. Unfortunately, we know little of the religion that led our early ancestors to build great stone monuments in sacred places. But it seems clear that the stones themselves played some vitally important part in the worship. The gigantic granite blocks of Stonehenge, of Baalbek in the Lebanon, and of a hundred other ancient temples were not dragged into position merely to satisfy the whim of some

Above: Sister Françoise, one of the most spectacular convulsionaires. She was actually crucified while in an ecstatic trance, and apparently suffered no permanent ill effects from the experience.

115

all-powerful ruler. They were apparently intended to be giant accumulators of magic power. In some strange way, this force was used. It is even possible that it was used to raise the stones into position.

How was this power harnessed? The answer must surely lie in some mysterious interaction between the forces of the earth and the powers of the subconscious mind. It may well be that a similar interaction occurred on a smaller scale in the cemetery of St. Medard. Medical science cannot explain how Gabrielle Moler resisted the blows of strong men and the heat of a blazing fire. We know that hypnosis can render people insensitive to pain, but it could not prevent Gabrielle Moler from being burned when she thrust her face and feet into the flames. Hypnotism alone cannot explain how a man loaded with heavy chains could bounce six feet into the air. We know that yogis possess these kinds of powers, but they are acquired only after years of arduous training. All we can say is that whatever occurred at St. Medard conferred extraordinary powers on the convulsionaires—or perhaps merely enabled them to make use of powers that all human beings possess.

Knowledge of the ancient religion of the forces of earth has been lost in the mists of time. Yet we have some fascinating clues to its nature. Anyone who wants seriously to follow them up should turn to an extraordinary and complex work called *The White Goddess*, written in the 1940s by the British poet Robert Graves. Graves describes how he was reading *The Mabinogion*, a collection of ancient Welsh legends, when he came across a curious and apparently meaningless poem called *The Song of Taliesin*. Suddenly, in a flash of inspiration, he realized that some of the most baffling lines of the poem were a series of medieval riddles, and that these riddles contained clues to an ancient Celtic system of knowledge. As he pursued his research into this knowledge, he discovered that it was not confined to Wales. It could be found in the poetry and mythology of ancient Greece, Phoenicia, Scandinavia, India, and Africa. *And it was always closely linked with the moon.*

This was in itself a fascinating insight, and it tied in with a theory put forward 20 years earlier by the anthropologist Margaret Murray. In the early 1920s, Dr. Murray had startled the academic world with a book called *The God of the Witches*. In it she had argued that what we now call witchcraft was actually an ancient pagan religion, whose chief deity was the moon goddess Diana. The ancient priests of Diana worshiped her by performing dances in which they wore animal skins and deer antlers on their heads. Christianity tried to stamp out this pagan religion, but it continued in secret. In Christian mythology, the antlered priest became the devil. In fact, he was a *shaman*, or magician-priest-doctor.

Graves came to an even more startling conclusion. He said that the ancients possessed a kind of knowledge based on intuition, on a certain oneness with Nature. This ancient knowledge sprang from the subconscious depths of the mind, and was symbolized by the moon.

When *The White Goddess* was published in 1948, many critics dismissed it as poetic fancy. Since then, however, an

Above: Margaret Murray, British Egyptologist and anthropologist who died in 1963. She presented the theory that witchcraft in Europe was actually a survival of an ancient pagan religion which worshiped the great mother goddess, the moon deity Diana.

Right: an ancient representation of the Horned God taken from the cave paintings in the cave of Les Trois Frères in Ariège, France, executed in palaeolithic times. He is the oldest known deity, from whom the Christian Devil inherited his traditional horns, clóven hooves, and tail.

Above: the poet Robert Graves in 1972. In his anthropological and mythological study *The White Goddess*, he claims that the ancient female, fertility, and mother goddess became the Muse of poetry, and that poetry itself began with the ritual worship of that goddess in early societies.

Below: performance of the Horn Dance is a tradition in Abbots Bromley, England. It is danced by six men holding antlers in front of them—perhaps in imitation of the ancient Horned God. Could this be a folk memory of prehistoric hunting rituals preserved as a traditional dance?

increasing number of scientific discoveries have supported Graves' ideas. Many scientists now accept that Stonehenge, Callanish, and other ancient monuments were intended as lunar observatories. The study of aboriginal tribes has confirmed the importance of the moon goddess and her connection with fertility rituals. In 1960 the anthropologist Charles Mountford studied tribes in the deserts of central Australia. He made a 300-mile journey with them to "centers of power," where certain rituals were performed. The ceremonies were designed to increase the life power of the worshippers, to stimulate the fertility of plants and animals, and to renew the sacred forces of the tribe. Mountford found that these centers of power lay on straight lines. Each tribe was responsible for looking after its own stretch of line, performing appropriate rituals to maintain its power. (According to students of dragon paths and leys, the lines of magnetic force do not remain permanently in the same place; they may change their location over the centuries, so that a holy place ceases to be holy.) Mountford observed that each center of power was marked by a rock, and the Australian aborigines painted serpents—or dragons—on the rocks to symbolize the mysterious life force. However, the aborigines insist that it is not the painting that has magical or religious properties, but *the rock itself.*

Modern science is only just beginning to uncover the ancient systems of knowledge. It is therefore hardly surprising to find that there are dozens of strange and conflicting theories on the subject. The Austrian engineer and cosmologist Hanns Horbiger, who died in 1931, recognized the significance of the moon in ancient legends. He concluded that the earth has had several moons, all of which finally crashed into the earth and caused vast catastrophes like the biblical flood and the destruction of Atlantis. He was convinced that our present moon is a huge block of ice—a theory we now know to be untrue. The witchcraft revival of recent years is based on the belief that witchcraft is an ancient fertility religion, and that its forces can be tapped today through the rituals performed at *Sabbats,* or gatherings of witches.

T. C. Lethbridge thought that Stonehenge and similar monuments might be giant markers set up for the guidance of aircraft or spacecraft. He also speculated that the moon might have been the scene of a great war between two rival planetary races—perhaps those of Venus and Mars—and that its craters were formed by atomic bombardment rather than by meteorites. We know that many of the moon's craters were created by some kind of impact rather than by volcanic activity because they sometimes overlap one another.

Lethbridge's theory sounds absurd. Yet in 1966 two moon satellites—America's Orbiter-2 and the Soviet's Lunar-9—both photographed groups of solid *structures* in two different places on the lunar surface. Ivan Sanderson writes: "The Lunar-9 photographs, taken on February 9, 1966, after the craft had landed in the Ocean of Storms, reveal two straight lines of equidistant stones that look like markers along an airport runway. These circular stones are all identical, and are

Left: aboriginal rock paintings in Charlies Creek, Queensland, Australia. The aborigines believe that magical or religious power lies in the rock itself rather than in their symbolic paintings.

positioned at an angle that produces a strong reflection from the sun, which would render them visible to a descending aircraft." The Soviet scientist Dr. S. Ivanov notes that "the objects, as seen in 3-D, seem to be arranged according to some definite geometric laws."

The Orbiter-2 photographs, taken some 2000 miles away from the Soviet site, show what appear to be eight pointed obelisks. From the angle of the sun and the length of its shadow, the largest of these objects was estimated to be about 75 feet high and 50 feet wide at the base. This makes it sound more like a tall pyramid than an obelisk. Moreover, the Soviet scientist Alexander Abramov states that the distribution of the Orbiter-2 objects is similar to the plan of the Egyptian pyramids

Above: a photograph by the Soviet moon satellite Luna 9, which landed in the Ocean of Storms, shows a curious row of stones. They seem too perfectly arranged to have happened by chance.

Right: the white cross photographed by astronomer Robert Curtiss in Alamogordo, New Mexico, in 1956. The arms, which cross each other at right angles, are each clearly several miles long.

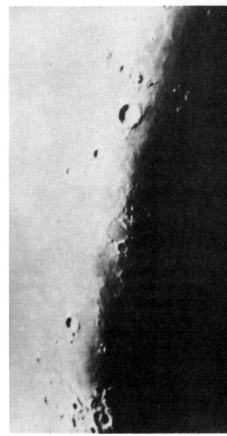

at Giza. A NASA official told Sanderson that the photographs were extremely clear, but explained that there had been "no speculation about them so far." He added that they had been filed.

On November 26, 1956 as American astronomer Robert E Curtiss was photographing the moon's surface through a 16-inch reflector telescope, he was startled to observe a white cross near the ring plan Fra Mauro. Each arm of the cross was several miles long. Scientists have been unable to explain this phenomenon.

John O'Neil, science editor of the New York *Herald Tribune* observed a gigantic bridgelike structure in the Sea of Crises. The sun shone *under* it when it was at a low angle, making it clearly visible. Other astronomers have since confirmed the existence of this giant "bridge" on the moon.

These observations bring to mind the vast system of artificial lines that can be seen in the arid valleys near Nazca in Peru These are a series of straight lines, interspersed with animal shapes and geometric patterns, that were carved in the ground

at some unknown date in the past. They look remarkably like landing strips for aircraft. They were not noticed until recent years because they can only be seen clearly from the air. The lines, which have been cut into the rocky floor of the valleys, extend for over 30 miles, sometimes crossing ravines or stopping in front of small mountains and reemerging absolutely straight on the other side. The most puzzling question is how the lines were kept so straight by men working at ground level, presumably without guidance from the air. There are enormous designs of disks, flowers, spiders, and birds, which were only revealed by aerial surveys. On an aerial photograph they look like markings made in the sand by a child. The difference is that they must have taken hundreds of people hundreds of hours to construct. For what purpose? Von Däniken is convinced that they were markings to guide spacecraft, and we have yet to find a more convincing explanation.

If future astronauts can verify that there are artificial structures on the moon, built by intelligent creatures, it would certainly be one of the most exciting discoveries in the history

Left: a Babylonian alabaster statuette of the moon goddess Astarte, dating from about 200 B.C. She was the most widely worshipped of all the deities of the ancient Middle East.

Below: a 17th-century engraving of moonstruck women dancing peculiarly in the town square. Women were considered particularly susceptible to the mysterious powers of the full moon's rays.

of the human race. Yet even this would do little to solve the really baffling enigmas about our satellite. For thousands of years, people accepted that the human mind is influenced by the moon just as surely as the tides are. Our word "lunatic" stems from the age-old belief in a connection between the moon and madness. Then came the Age of Reason. Scientists and philosophers pointed out that the idea of a link between humans and the moon is absurd. How could a planetary body a quarter of a million miles away influence the human mind? It was a good point; but it was unsound. Modern research has shown that not only human beings, but also all kinds of animals, are affected by the moon. Oysters open and close their shells according to the rhythm of the tides, and it had always been assumed that this activity was the result of tidal movement alone. Dr. Frank A. Brown, Professor of Biology at Northwestern University, found it to be otherwise. When he moved some oysters to a closed tank in the laboratory, away from the tidal influences, he discovered that they appear to open and close their shells in direct response to the movements of the moon.

The police have observed that crimes of violence tend to increase at the time of the full moon. One report from the Philadelphia Police Department stated that "people whose antisocial behavior had psychotic roots—such as firebugs, kleptomaniacs, destructive drivers, and homicidal alcoholics— seemed to go on the rampage as the moon rounded, calming down as the moon waned." Nurses in mental institutions are familiar with the rise in violence and tension that occurs among their patients when the moon is full. Most family physicians in country areas, where the doctor-patient re- lationship tends to be closer and longer-lasting than in towns, can tell of people whose behavior becomes eccentric at the time of the full moon. A doctor in the area where I live in Cornwall tells me he never expects to get an undisturbed night's sleep when the moon is full, and that there are far more cases of wife-beating and battered babies at that time.

How, then, does the moon affect the human mind? The answer may lie in electrical forces. Scientists now know that the phases of the moon bring about modulations in the earth's electrical and magnetic fields. When Harold Burr of Yale University connected delicate voltameters to trees, he discovered that the electrical fields of the trees varied according to the seasons, to the activity of sunspots, and to the phases of the moon. The same delicate voltameters connected to human beings are able to tell when women ovulate, and when people are suffering from cancer. It would therefore appear that human health is tied up with certain electrical forces in the body. The Chinese believe that these forces run in lines beneath the surface of the body, and the points at which they join are acupuncture points. Practitioners of acupuncture treat illness by stimulating these points with wooden splinters or metal needles. Western television teams have filmed surgical opera- tions in China conducted on wide-awake patients who have been "anesthetized" by means of one, or a few, needles in- serted into the skin at acupuncture points. The patients

Right: the lines of acupuncture points on the human body. The Chinese acupuncturists believe that bodily forces run in lines beneath the surface of the skin, and the points at which they join are acupuncture points. The lines themselves are related to the "dragon paths" of force that cross the surface of the earth.

Far right: modern acupuncture as practiced at the Tsung I Yen hospital in Peking. About 40 per- cent of the hospitals in China give acupuncture treatment only.

Right: an operation in Shanghai, in which the patient is anesthe- sized only by the traditional method of acupuncture. Westerners who have witnessed such operations have been impressed by the fact that the patient seems to be completely free of any pain.

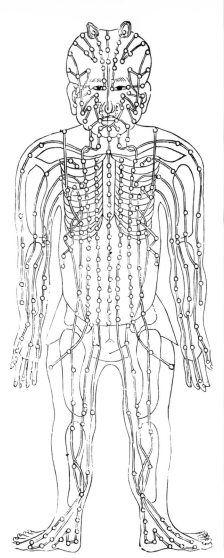
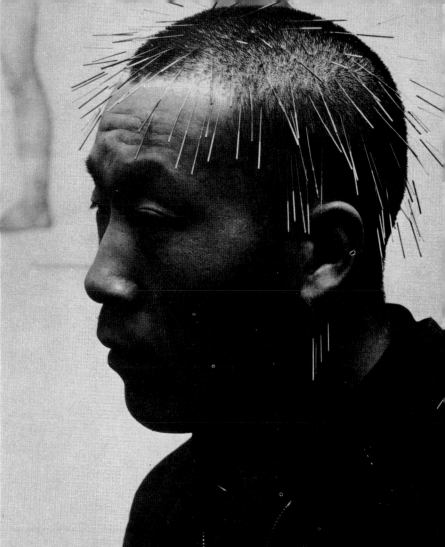
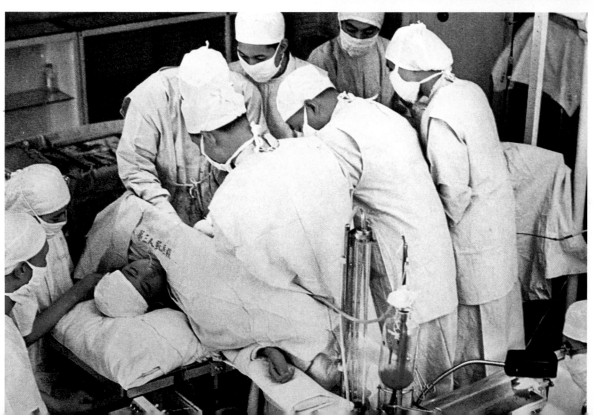

Above: the weeping sarcophagus of Arles-sur-Tech, France, consistently produces about two pints of water every day—and modern science can't say how.

Left: an 18th-century engraving showing visitors to the strange sarcophagus. It became a kind of healing shrine, and the water is still claimed to have healing properties for the faithful.

appeared to feel no pain, and one of them smiled and joked as a tumor was removed from his stomach.

Acupuncture works, and it is gaining wider acceptance in the West. But Western science has not yet accepted the Chinese belief that the "meridians," or lines of force, that run through the human body are of basically the same nature as the dragon paths that extend over the earth. This seems altogether more difficult for the pragmatic Western intellect to acknowledge. After all, the earth is not a living creature.

Or is it? Sir Arthur Conan Doyle, the creator of Sherlock Holmes, once wrote a short novel called *The Day the Earth Screamed*. In it the hero, Professor Challenger, reaches the startling conclusion that the earth is alive. To prove his theory he drills a deep shaft through the earth's surface, and drops

Above: a drawing of the revered reliquary in the chapel of San Gennaro in Naples. It is said to hold the saint's blood, shed during his martyrdom in A.D. 305. During important religious festivals, the blood mysteriously liquifies from its normal black mass and takes on the appearance of fresh blood. In spite of many investigations, there is no satisfactory scientific explanation.

an enormous stake down it. The earth convulses and screams. In the light of modern knowledge, this idea is not so wildly improbable as it sounds. The earth has its fields of force just as human beings have. We speak of life-fields in human beings. Why not in the case of the earth? Perhaps the earth is not alive in the same sense that we are. But if some investigators are right, it often behaves as if it were.

This theory would offer an explanation of why certain spots on the earth's surface seem to be blessed, while others are cursed. When skeptics read stories of miracles at holy places like Lourdes in France, Compostella in Spain, and Holywell in Wales, they are inclined to fall back on the explanation that faith, like hypnosis, can produce miraculous effects on the mind and body. Certainly most reports of amazing cures could be accounted for in this way. But some of the most astounding miracles involve things rather than people. Outside the old church of Arles-sur-Tech in southern France stands a marble sarcophagus that weeps—to the bafflement of modern science. It would probably be more accurate to say that the marble sweats. When the heavy lid of the sarcophagus is removed, water is seen to form in its inner surface. Usually the slab is held in place with iron bands. There is a small hole, large enough to insert a pipette, in the top edge of the sarcophagus. Through this hole the sarcophagus yields up on average about two pints of water per day. This water is reputed to have healing properties, and does not evaporate if left in an open vessel. In the past, the flow of water has amounted to many gallons at a time—more than the cubic capacity of the sarcophagus. There is no spring near the coffin, and the mystery cannot be explained by condensation. It is just another of those unsolved enigmas associated with holy places and objects.

The same is true of two bottles of blood that are kept in a small chapel next to Naples cathedral. It is the blood of St. Januarius, who was martyred in A.D. 305. Three times a year the blackened mass in the bottle changes color, and takes on the appearance of normal fresh blood. This has happened thousands of times—always on three religious feasts celebrated in May, September, and December. Careful investigation has revealed no evidence of trickery.

What is perhaps equally significant is that there have been occasions when the blood failed to liquefy. Why should that be so? The most plausible explanation is that the liquefaction somehow involves the faith of the worshippers, and that if this is insufficient to trigger the strange psycho-chemical reaction required, nothing happens. However, it is also possible that the earth forces that animate the spot are less strong at some times than at others. It would be interesting to have full astronomical data for the periods when the liquefaction failed to take place, and so be able to determine the exact position of the moon and the planets at the time.

But what would be most interesting of all would be to understand the laws that govern the interaction between the vital forces of the earth and the vital forces of our subconscious. If we could discover that secret, we would have taken the first great step toward recovery of the lost knowledge of the ancients.

8

Creatures from Other Worlds

In February 1855 England was in the grip of an exceptionally icy winter. Even the West Country, where winters are seldom severe, was covered with a blanket of frozen snow. On the morning of February 8 Albert Brailford, the school principle of Topsham village in Devonshire, was intrigued to see a line of peculiar prints in the snow when he walked out of his front door. The prints were shaped like horseshoes, each about four inches long, and looked like they might have been made by a hoofed animal. The strange thing was that the prints were in a completely straight line, one in front of the other. It was as though the animal had

A single straight line of tracks in the snow—just one of the odd pieces of evidence that suggests there are creatures around us more extraordinary than we suspect. Right: the peculiar footprints discovered in Devonshire one snowy morning in February 1855.

Right: a hooved Devil dancing in one of Goya's paintings of witches. The strange Devonshire hoof-marks were promptly and fearfully identified as the Devil's prints.

"Even Londoners had to admit that it was a strange story"

been treading an invisible tightrope on its hind legs. Brailford followed the tracks along the street, and pointed them out to various acquaintances. The villagers agreed that the prints were unlike those of any known animal. As they tracked them through the fresh snow, the mystery deepened. The tracks stopped at a high garden wall, *and continued on the other side*. Yet the snow on top of the wall was undisturbed. It seemed that the creature had jumped the wall with one bound, or walked straight through it.

All along the South Devon coast for 40 miles people discovered more of the mysterious tracks. In some places they went over rooftops. In one village they stopped at the door of a shed and reappeared at the back of it, emerging from a six-inch hole. The prints went up to a haystack, disappeared, and resumed on the other side. They stopped at one end of a drainpipe lying on the ground, and started again at the far end. The tracks always lay in a straight line, although they often doubled back on themselves.

News traveled slowly in those days. It was more than a week before Londoners learned of the sensational events in Devonshire. City sophisticates smiled at accounts of old ladies locking themselves in cottages while men armed with pitchforks and shotguns searched yards and barns for some unknown creature. They were amused at the country dwellers' belief that the tracks were the "Devil's footprints." To city dwellers it sounded like a typical rural storm-in-a-teacup. They surmised that the prints had been made by some animal, and that the superstitious country folk had interpreted them as the marks of the Devil himself. However, when more precise information began to appear, even Londoners had to admit that it was a strange story.

A Devon vicar and naturalist, who denied that there was a supernatural explanation, carefully measured the distance between the prints. He found it always to be exactly eight and a half inches. A fellow villager some distance away had measured the tracks in his garden, and also found them to be eight and a half inches apart. From this it appeared that there was only one creature involved. The oddest part was that the tracks extended over 40 miles of coastline and, allowing for detours and deviations, extended for more than twice that distance. What small animal, if there was only one, could walk over 80 miles between dusk and dawn, climbing over roofs, and leaping over or walking through haystacks?

A famous naturalist, Sir Richard Owen, examined sketches of the tracks, and asserted that the prints had been made by a badger. Owen's badger presumably walked on its hind legs.

The likeliest explanation seemed to be that the tracks were made as a joke by some local prankster. But even supposing he wore special shoes with horseshoes attached to the soles, how did he vault walls, stride over rooftops, and cover 80 miles or so in a single night?

One of the correspondents of the *London Illustrated News* drew attention to a report made by the British explorer Sir James Ross in May 1840. Ross had anchored off the desolate Kerguelen Island in the Antarctic, and had been intrigued to

Below: Sir Richard Owen, who was a well-known 19th-century naturalist. He explained the Devonshire footprints as having been made by a group of badgers. He maintained that those who said it had been a single creature that made all the footprints had simply not gone over the ground with "acute and unbiassed observation."

find hoofprints in the snow. His party followed them for some distance until they vanished on rocky ground. There are no ponies on Kerguelen Island, or any other animal that could have made such prints.

The London *Times* for March 14, 1840 contains an account of mysterious tracks in the Scottish Highlands. They had been followed for 12 miles through the snow near Glenorchy, and they sound identical to the Devil's footprints in Devon. They were shaped like horseshoes, but gave the impression that the creature who made them had been bounding or leaping rather than trotting.

There are many accounts of Devil's hoofprints in old chronicles, but skeptical historians have been inclined to treat them as superstitious inventions. A typical example may be found in the *Chronicum* of the Benedictine monk Flavellus of Épernay, France. Describing a wild tempest that occurred in A.D. 943 he writes that, "demons or horses were seen at the height of the storm." Abbot Ralph of Coggeshall Abbey in Essex, England, records that after a tremendous storm in July 1205, "certain monstrous tracks were seen in several places, of a kind never seen before. Men said they were the prints of demons." No doubt many of these old stories are either inventions or exaggerations or an actual event. But couldn't some of these ancient chroniclers have been recording visitations similar to the one in Devon?

One explanation of the Devon prints was suggested by Morris K. Jessup, the ufologist who died in mysterious circumstances in 1959. Predictably, Jessup believed that the tracks were made by some kind of flying craft. He draws attention to the report of one observer that the prints were so clear-cut that they seemed to have been stamped into the snow "as if made by a drill or mechanical frame." Jessup suggests that the marks could have been made by a low-flying craft that maintained its

Above: Kerguelen Island in the Antarctic, visited by a British expedition in 1840. They found a set of inexplicable hoofprints.

Below: James Clark Ross, the famous arctic explorer who was the leader of the 1840 expedition.

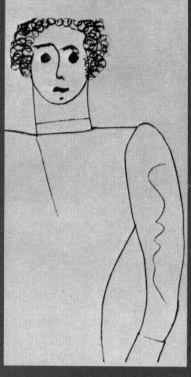

Above: three drawings made by a young girl, Mary Barnes, who was brought to Dr. Albert Wilson in 1896. During two years of treatment, she manifested ten separate personalities known as B1 to B10. She made the sketch on the left as B10 who seemed to be blind and imbecilic but could draw by touch. If an obstacle were placed between her eyes and her drawing, it made no difference to the rapidity or accuracy of her work. The middle drawing was drawn by B3, a normal but exceedingly mischievous girl whom her parents nicknamed "Old Nick." The picture on the right was executed by B6, the stable personality that finally emerged and remained permanent. As B6, Mary Barnes was normal—except that she had no memory of any event or experience before this personality emerged about halfway through her illness.

distance from the ground by some kind of energy beam such as radar. This would certainly explain how the prints continued over rooftops and passed over walls and haystacks. Yet it fails to explain why the tracks often doubled back on themselves.

Some ufologists have suggested that UFOs may originate in another dimension—a space-time world running parallel to our own that may contain living creatures, just as our world does. David Lang, the Tennessee farmer who disappeared without trace, may have fallen into this parallel dimension. If he could unwittingly fall into their dimension, why should not creatures from the parallel world accidently fall into ours? One of the most remarkable things about the Devil's footprints in Devon is that they wandered around for so many miles, as if the creature who made them were looking for something. They strayed over or through walls and across rooftops as if their owners were unfamiliar with our world.

It is interesting to note that the stories of demonic activity from Flavellus and Abbot Ralph both involve extremely violent storms, when electrical activity would have been unusually powerful. Remembering the strange behavior of compasses in the Bermuda Triangle and other Devil's grave-yards, is it not conceivable that unusual magnetic fields might create a bridge between this world and a parallel universe?

It is now time to pause and survey some of the ground we have covered. As we look back over the mysteries considered in this book, we have to admit that no single explanation, or set of explanations, can accommodate all these strange phenomena. Besides, there are many other types of enigmas that have not even been discussed. To touch briefly on a few, let us look first at poltergeist phenomena. In a famous case that took place in Amherst, Nova Scotia, in 1878 Esther Cox was the center of poltergeist manifestations. Objects flew through the air, spontaneous fires broke out, and an invisible spirit wrote on a wall: "Esther, you are mine to kill." Several witnesses were present with the young girl when the threat was written.

Then there is the closely related subject of demonic possession. When a possessed woman was exorcised by Theophilus Reisinger in Iowa in 1928, her body tore itself loose from the grip of several nuns who were trying to hold her down, rose through the air, and clung to the wall of the room close to the ceiling. Hundreds of similar cases have been recorded, some by modern psychologists. If these phenomena are caused by outside forces, it would certainly appear that such forces can sometimes be hostile to us human beings. It is of course possible that the forces originate in our own subconscious mind. In this case, the problem is equally baffling, because it suggests that a human being may possess several different personalities at different levels. There have been many astonishing cases of multiple personalities in which a person has suddenly lost his or her memory and been taken over by another personality. The second character has then performed actions that are completely foreign to the normal personality. In *Sybil*, a book by Flora Schreiber, the woman Sybil was taken over by no less than 16 personalities. In which world do these personalities exist? Is the world of the subconscious mind one of the parallel worlds we have been discussing?

In a book called *Superminds*, the British physicist John Taylor discusses people like Uri Geller and Matthew Manning, who can bend spoons merely by stroking them and cause metal to fracture without even touching it. Taylor has observed many such psychics, including young children, in his laboratory. He has concluded that there is no trickery involved in their ability to bend metal or move objects at a distance. It is his opinion that their powers stem from some mysterious force, akin to magnetism, which is probably also involved in poltergeist activity. If the force of a child's mind can move small objects around Taylor's laboratory, is it not conceivable that a similar force might have been harnessed to raise the 1000-ton granite blocks of the temple at Baalbeck, or the immense monoliths of Stonehenge?

The hypothesis that we are simply dealing with unknown and impersonal forces that may originate in the human subconscious leaves far too many mysteries unexplained. It would not account for people vanishing without trace, nor the opposite of this— the appearance of mysterious strangers in our world.

In the 11th century, two extraordinary children walked out of a cave at a place called Woolpit in Suffolk, England. The chronicler Abbot Ralph of Coggeshall describes them as follows: "They had all their members like those of other men, but in the color of their skin, they differed from all other mortals of our earth." Both children were green.

The boy grew sick and died, but the girl survived and slowly

The Green Children

One day in August 1887 near the small village of Banjos, Spain, a boy and girl walked out of a cave. Some peasants working in a field saw them, and were utterly amazed. The two children had skin as green as grass!

When seen closer, the children were found to have almond-shaped eyes of an Asiatic type. They could not speak Spanish, and they wore clothes of a material never before seen in the Spain of the 19th century. No one could understand their language, and no one could analyze the fabric. For five days the boy and girl would not eat any of the various foods brought to them. Finally they began to eat beans. By then the boy was so weakened that he died, but the girl survived. The green color of her skin gradually faded.

After learning some Spanish, the girl described the country she came from and how she had left it. Her story only made the mystery deeper. She said her native land had no sun at all, and was separated from a sunny land by a river. One day a sudden whirlwind had lifted her and the boy and deposited them in the cave.

The green girl of Banjos lived for only five years more. The mystery of how she and the boy had appeared in Spain was never solved.

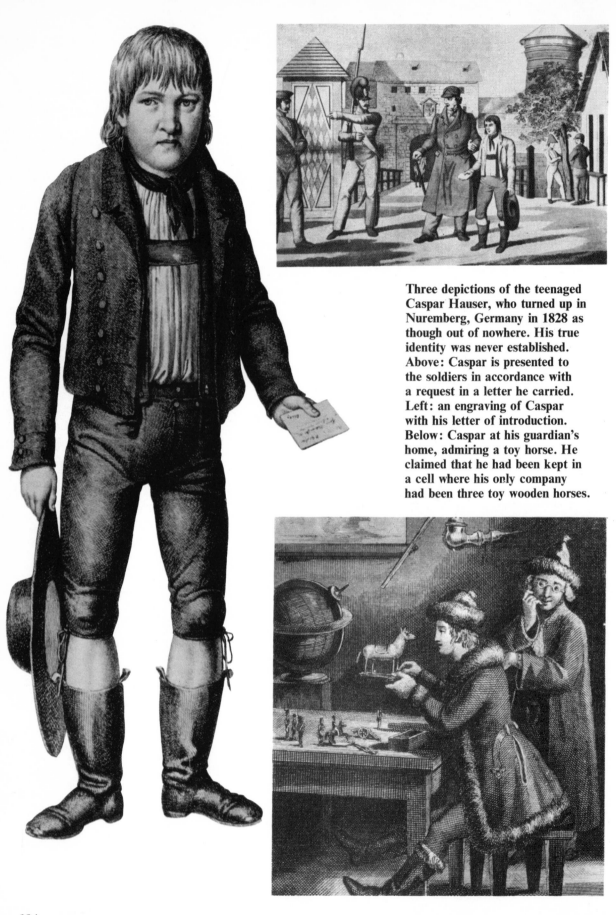

Three depictions of the teenaged Caspar Hauser, who turned up in Nuremberg, Germany in 1828 as though out of nowhere. His true identity was never established. Above: Caspar is presented to the soldiers in accordance with a request in a letter he carried. Left: an engraving of Caspar with his letter of introduction. Below: Caspar at his guardian's home, admiring a toy horse. He claimed that he had been kept in a cell where his only company had been three toy wooden horses.

learned English. When she could talk, she explained that she and the boy had come from a land where there was no sunlight. One day they had wandered into a cavern while looking after sheep, and had lost their way. When they emerged into the unaccustomed sunlight of a strange world, they were terrified. The children had at first refused all food except green beans. The girl became used to other foods, however, and her skin slowly lost its green tint.

The most famous case of a strange person appearing in mysterious circumstances is that of Caspar Hauser. On May 26, 1828 a shambling teenage boy wandered into the Unschlitt Square in Nuremberg, Germany. Trembling and mumbling incoherently, he accosted a shoemaker and offered him a letter. When he was taken to the police station, another letter was found in his pocket. One letter purported to be from his mother, who said that the boy's name was Caspar, and that his father had been a soldier. The other was apparently from a poor laborer who had brought up the boy, and who asked that he be taken into the army. It was quickly established that both letters were fakes, written by the same person probably to cover up the boy's identity.

Asked to write his name, the boy wrote "Caspar Hauser." He was able to mumble a few words, but otherwise gave the impression of being imbecilic. It soon became clear, however, that Hauser was not an imbecile. Although he seemed totally ignorant of the world and of even the most everyday objects in it, he began to learn with a rapidity that proved he was highly intelligent. Within a few months, Caspar Hauser had learned enough German to explain what he knew of his former life. He said that for as long as he could recall, he had lived in a tiny cell. When he awoke, he found bread and water on the floor. Sometimes the water tasted bitter, and after drinking it he fell into a deep sleep. When he woke up, he had been washed and his nails had been cut. He was not unhappy because he knew no other way of life.

Handbills were sent out all over Germany to try to establish the boy's identity, but no one was able to throw light on the mystery. Professor Georg Daumer, who became Hauser's guardian, discovered that the boy had an unusually acute sense of smell, could see in the dark, and found daylight painful to his eyes—all of which seemed to confirm his story.

In October 1829 Hauser was found unconscious and bleeding on the floor of Daumer's celler. He had been attacked by an unknown assailant who had struck him down with a club, and possibly also tried to stab him.

During the next four years, Hauser had a number of guardians. Finally an Englishman, Lord Charles Stanhope, moved him from Nuremberg to the nearby town of Ansbach in Bavaria. On December 14, 1833 Hauser staggered into his house, bleeding heavily from a stab wound in his ribs. He explained that a laborer had brought him a message asking him to meet someone in the Hofgarten. There a man with dark whiskers and a black cloak had asked him, "Are you Caspar Hauser?" When he said yes, the man handed him a silk purse, and then stabbed him in the side. The purse was found in the Hofgarten, and

Above: Stephanie de Beauharnais and her daughter Princess Louise. Stephanie, Duchess of Bade, was one of the many noble women mentioned as Caspar's mother by a public wildly intrigued by the mystery. Caspar was alleged to be the bastard son of every high-born rake of the period, and the offspring of virtually the entire Catholic Church hierarchy from the pope himself down. Like all the other circumstances of the Caspar Hauser tale, nobody knows to this day what the truth was.

contained an incoherent note signed M.L.O. It said that Hauser would be able to identify his assailant, who came from a place on the Bavarian border. The name of the place was illegible. Hauser died on December 17, 1833 without having been able to throw any light on the identity of his murderer.

From the moment of his appearance in Nuremberg, controversy had raged around Caspar Hauser. There were many theories as to his origins, but most people believed that he was the illegitimate son of some noble family, and had been kept a prisoner to conceal the dishonor until he became too big to remain locked away. Jacques Bergier, French writer on the occult, has another theory that is shared by many students of enigmas. It would explain the mysterious appearance of the green children as well as that of Caspar Hauser. Bergier suggests that, for many centuries, the earth has been under study by certain extraterrestrial intelligences. "In my opinion," he says, "after the period of simply auditing and recording what happened on earth, came another period, beginning a few centuries ago, in which the Intelligences began to conduct experiments. These experiments consist of introducing beings capable of arousing the most diverse reactions into our midst, and then studying the way we react—the way we study the behavior of rats in artificial labyrinths."

It is a suggestion worthy of Charles Fort. And, however great our revulsion at the idea of being treated as laboratory rats, it would certainly be hard to find a more all-embracing solution to the unexplained. Indeed, the chief objection to this theory is that it sounds *too* neat and easy. Any strange event can be explained by assuming that extraterrestrial intelligences wanted to study our reactions, and so deliberately engineered some incident that would baffle us.

There are, however, other mysteries that, if they do not contradict the extraterrestrial hypothesis, certainly challenge us to

Above: Lord Stanhope, the English nobleman known throughout Europe for his eccentricity. He took a personal interest in Caspar and visited him from time to time. Then, at the point when the boy's presence in Nuremberg had created a great controversy because of conjecture over his birth, Lord Stanhope removed him to Ansbach. He put Caspar in the care of a teacher and a soldier.

Above: a letter written by Caspar and some drawings that he is supposed to have produced. Some skeptical observers have pointed out that the drawings are very sophisticated for a boy who was an illiterate until he was 17.

Right: the first attempt on Caspar's life. He claimed he was attacked by a man in dark clothing wearing leather gloves and a silk mask. The attacker struck Caspar and fled, leaving him unconscious in the cellar of the house.

Left: Caspar Hauser as he was in 1830, two years after he had appeared in Nuremberg. By this time he spoke fluently, had learned to read and write, and could handle everyday utensils just as well as any other adult.

Right: the monument marking the spot where Caspar was fatally stabbed in an Ansbach park. The Latin inscription says, "On this place for mysterious reasons one mysterious figure was murdered by another mysterious figure."

Above and right: trees devastated by the explosion of a meteor in Siberia in 1908. They were a considerable distance from the Stoney Tunguska River where the meteor struck—and vanished like a huge bomb instead of fragmenting the way meteors usually do.

look for different possibilities. Two examples come to mind.

On June 17, 1908 an enormous meteor was seen to streak across the sky in Siberia. It struck the earth with a tremendous explosion near the Stoney Tunguska River. The explosion was heard for 600 miles around, and two villages were wiped out. But Siberia is a vast and barren land, and the government of the time had more to worry about than meteors—the country was seething with political discontent that led to the 1917 Revolution. In 1927 a scientific expedition penetrated the roadless terrain near the site of the explosion, and found that an area of 400 square miles had been devastated. The odd thing was that this meteor had not behaved like others. Instead of splitting into fragments as it hit earth, it had vanished like a huge bomb.

Later expeditions to the area also failed to solve the mystery. In 1975 a team of Soviet scientists concluded that the devastation had been caused by the tail of a comet that had struck the earth. However, students of enigmas point to an earlier finding that the soil in the devastated area was highly radioactive. It was as if a huge atomic bomb had exploded. Of course, atomic bombs do not streak across the sky. But UFOs do, according to all the evidence. Was it an atom-powered flying saucer that exploded over Siberia? If so, and if it was constructed by Bergier's extraterrestrial Intelligences, these beings are evidently less infallible than Bergier seems to suppose. Unless, of course, they created the explosion by some highly sophisticated means of remote control simply to see how people on earth would react.

If the aim of the extraterrestrials is to stimulate human beings for psychological study, it is hard to see what they achieved by disturbing a mausoleum on the island of Barbados. The Chase family tomb, which stands in a churchyard above Oistin's Bay,

is constructed of stone blocks held together by cement, and is closed by a marble door. It was built in 1724 by a plantation owner, and his wife was the first to be entombed. It was not re-opened until 1807, when the coffin of family member Thomasina Goddard was placed in it. The next year the massive marble door was opened again to receive the coffin of Mary Chase. She was the daughter of Thomas Chase, one of the most hated men in Barbados. In 1812 another of Chase's daughters, Dorcas, was buried in the tomb. According to rumor, Dorcas Chase had died through her father's ill-treatment.

A month later Thomas Chase himself died. When the tomb was opened to receive his body, some of the coffins were found to be disarranged. Mary Chase's coffin had been thrown across the tomb and stood upside down, and Thomasina Goddard's coffin was lying on its side. The family was indignant, assuming that hostile plantation workers were responsible. Other people were less certain. They knew it was unlike the superstitious Barbadians to disturb the dead. Besides, the marble door slab was heavy, and would have taken several men to remove it. Why would they have gone to all that trouble merely to overturn two coffins? The coffins were put in their proper places, and the vault was carefully sealed.

Four years later in 1816 the tomb was reopened for the interment of another child, Samuel Ames. It was discovered that all the coffins had been hurled about the vault. But the cement holding the great slab in place had been found undisturbed.

Two months later Samuel Ames' father died. A curious crowd accompanied the funeral procession to the tomb. When it was opened they were not disappointed. Once again the coffins had been thrown around the vault—with the single exception of

The Unexplained Blast Over Nevada

On the night of April 18, 1962 at about 7:30 p.m. an explosion ripped across the Nevada sky. The flash was as bright as an atomic blast, and the noise shook the earth for miles. Was it an atom bomb test? A meteor? An enemy missile or aircraft? These logical questions were never answered by those who investigated the incident.

The first report of an odd UFO had come from Oneida, New York. Observers there saw a glowing red object moving west at a great altitude. It was too slow to be a missile, too high to be a plane. A meteor was ruled out because this object was tracked by radar, and meteors cannot be. As it moved west across the country, reports of it came in from the states of Kansas, Utah, Montana, New Mexico, Wyoming, Arizona, and California.

At some point the huge UFO landed near an electric power station in Eureka, Utah. Until it took off again, in its own time, the station was unable to operate at all.

The possibility that the explosion was from a nuclear test was denied by the Atomic Energy Commission. Its spokesmen said there was no atomic testing anywhere on the North American continent at that time.

Jet interceptors from the Air Defense Command pursued the UFO, but radar screens lost it about 70 miles northwest of Las Vegas. It was in that precise direction that the blast took place somewhere above the Mesquite Range.

Few people in the United States ever learned about this unusual event. Only the Las Vegas *Sun*, which was in the area of the explosion, carried the story. The news was otherwise suppressed by the Air Force.

Above: the Chase family vault on the island of Barbados as it is today—completely empty inside. For many years the coffins in the vault were found in disarray everytime the mausoleum was re-opened to receive another dead member of the important family, although it was always sealed. The governor of the island finally ordered the removal and burial of the coffins elsewhere in 1820 after the "haunted tomb" had become the object of sightseeing.

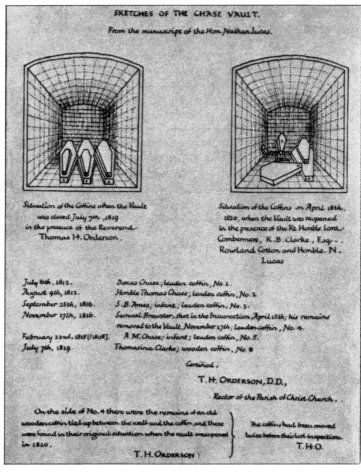

SKETCHES OF THE CHASE VAULT.

From the manuscript of the Hon. Nathan Lucas.

Situation of the Coffins when the Vault was closed July 7th ,1819 in the presence of the Reverend Thomas H. Orderson.

Situation of the Coffins on April 18th, 1820, when the Vault was reopened in the presence of the Rt. Honble Lord Combermere, R.B.Clarke, Esqr., Rowland Cotton and Honble. N. Lucas

July 6th , 1812.	Dorcas Chase; leaden coffin, No.1.
August 9th, 1812.	Honble Thomas Chase; leaden coffin, No.2.
September 25th, 1816.	S.B.Ames; infant; leaden coffin, No.3.
November 17th, 1816.	Samuel Brewster, shot in the Insurrection, April 15th; his remains removed to the Vault, November 17th; leaden coffin, No.4.
February 22nd, 1818 (?1808).	A.M.Chase; infant; leaden coffin, No.5.
July 7th, 1819.	Thomasina Clarke; wooden coffin, No.6

Certified,

T. H. ORDERSON, D.D.,

Rector of the Parish of Christ Church.

On the side of No.4 there were the remains of an old wooden coffin tied up between the wall and the coffin, and these were found in their original situation when the vault was opened in 1820.

The coffins had been moved twice before their last inspection. T. H. O.

T. H. ORDERSON

Right: drawings by Nathan Lucas, an eyewitness, which show how the coffins were originally arranged and how they were discovered to be when the Chase tomb was opened on April 18, 1820. It was after this that the strange tomb was abandoned.

140

Mrs. Goddard's. The Reverend Thomas Orderson conducted a careful search of the vault in an attempt to find the explanation. The tomb was dry and sound. There were no cracks either in the walls or floor. The seal of the door had not been broken.

The tomb was elaborately resealed. Three years later in July 1819 enormous crowds arrived to watch the interment of Mrs. Thomasina Clarke. They saw five men chip off the cement from the slab, which was designed to open inward. Even when the cement had been removed, the slab seemed hard to move. The reason became clear when it had been shifted by main force. The leaden coffin of Thomas Chase lay against the door. The other coffins were once more in disarray—again with the exception of Mrs. Goddard's.

After the vault had been searched in vain for any sign of intruders, the coffins were replaced, and white sand scattered all over the floor. The slab was again cemented into place, and then sealed with private seals.

During the following months visitors flocked to see the "haunted tomb." In April 1820 Sir Stapleton Cotton, the Governor of Barbados, became so curious about it that he decided to have it inspected. The seals were intact. But when the massive slab was moved, the usual disorder prevailed. Coffins had tumbled all over the vault. Mrs. Goddard's coffin—now little more than a bundle of planks secured by wire—was the only one that was undisturbed. The sand on the floor bore no sign of footprints. The Governor decided that the strange affair was becoming a disgrace to the island. He ordered the coffins to be removed and buried. And from that day to this, the vault has remained empty.

None of the normal explanations is acceptable. An earthquake, to which the area is subject occasionally, would not account for the fact that Mrs. Goddard's coffin always remained unmoved. A member of the Ames family believed that the answer lay in giant puffballs, a type of fungus that grows in caves in Honduras. These puffballs can reach a diameter of 20 feet, and can lift rocks by their thrust as they grow. On reaching their full growth they explode and disintegrate into powder. This explanation is improbable for many reasons. For one, Honduras is 2000 miles from Barbados. For another, puffballs had not been observed on the island. Finally, there were no cracks in the tomb for puffball spores to enter even if they had reached Barbados, and witnesses saw no sign of fungus between the stones.

It seems probably that, in this case, we are dealing with a mixture of poltergeist activity and haunting, centered around the coffin of the hated Thomas Chase. It would have been interesting to see what would have happened if Sir Stapleton Cotton had removed only Thomas Chase's coffin, resealed the tomb, and investigated it again later.

Clearly it seems unlikely that Bergier's extraterrestrials were involved in this curious mystery. But even as a haunting it was unusual. Normally poltergeist activities only take place in the presence of living human beings, as if they had to draw energy from a living person—or, as a psychologist might say, as if their energy originated in the subconscious mind. There have been

Above: Sir Stapleton Cotton, the governor of Barbados in 1820. He decided that the Chase family mausoleum should be abandoned. Below: Sir Arthur Conan Doyle, one of the numerous investigators to attempt a solution of the mystery of the Chase tomb. His suggestion was that a combustive force had been created inside the tomb and had tossed around its contents. This force came from what he called the "effluvia" of slaves in combination with some unnamed forces.

cases in which poltergeists have persisted in the same house over a long period while a series of tenants have come and gone. This suggests that the poltergeist may be some kind of independent entity, a spirit, that needs to borrow energy before it can make itself heard or felt. There were plenty of human beings to supply energy for poltergeist activity in the area of the Chase family tomb. Many were simple peasants who were terrified of the phenomena. Their fear may have increased the psychic vibrations that led to the disturbances.

We must indulge in one more speculation in our attempt to formulate some general theory to cover enigmas and mysteries. The disappearance of Lang, Bathurst, and others suggest that there may be parallel worlds in our universe. Perhaps these worlds do not exist in other dimensions, but only on other energy levels. Perhaps they can intermingle like the different levels of matter—solids, liquids, and gases—do in our world, as in a syphon of soda water, for example. If we look back over the scientific history of the past few hundred years—from Galileo to Einstein, from electricity to black holes—we cannot lightly dismiss Lethbridge's hypothesis that we live in a multi-level universe in which our reality is only one of many.

This book has been about the *interaction* of these levels of reality. Some people seem to have slipped through a "crack" in our reality into another world. Some phenomena—including poltergeists, UFOs, and lake monsters—seem to have slipped from some other level of reality into our world. It seems possible that certain types of powerful electrical phenomena are able to link the two worlds—and for all we know, the results may be as startling and incomprehensible to the inhabitants of these other worlds as they are to us. There is also a certain amount of evidence that some part of us—the psychic part—already has a bridge to other levels. This may be why certain people can foretell the future, or describe a crime simply by holding some object associated with it. Thought evidently has far more power than we give it credit for. It may be able to stamp itself on objects, leaving an imprint that remains for thousands of years. Some of the unknown forces we are trying to understand may be evil. Their thoughts may be able to evoke evil reality, as in the case of curses.

Imagine a book of unexplained mysteries written by a contemporary of Shakespeare. It might include the mystery of the falling stars that sweep through the sky foretelling disaster; the mystery of the Kraken, the giant sea devil with 50-foot tentacles; the mystery of monster bones, sometimes found in caves or on beaches. Such a book would be a curious mixture of truth and absurdity, fact and legend. We would all feel superior as we turned its pages and murmured: "Of course, they didn't know about comets and giant squids and dinosaurs." If *this* book should happen to find its way into the hands of our remote descendants, they may smile pityingly and say: "It's incredible to think that they knew nothing about epsilon fields or multiple psychic feedback or cross gravitational energies. They didn't even know about the ineluctability of time." But let us hope that such a descendant is in a charitable mood, and might add: "And yet they managed to ask a few of the right questions."

Right: *Not to be Reproduced* by the Belgian surrealist painter René Magritte. The surprise of this portrait is the impossible reflection in the mirror of the same view rather than of the face. Perhaps the surrealists' lesson for us is that we should not take everything for granted in the world we think we know.

Picture Credits